D1015078

Keeping Free

Keeping Free

Frank Pollard

BROADMAN PRESS
Nashville, Tennessee

4252-16
ISBN: 0-8054-5216-8

Unless otherwise indicated, Scripture quotations are from the Revised Standard Version of the Bible, copyrighted 1946, 1952, © 1971, 1973.

Quotations marked NASB are from the *New American Standard Bible*. Copyright © The Lockman Foundation, 1960, 1962, 1963, 1971, 1972, 1973, 1975. Used by permission.

Quotations marked GNB are from the *Good News Bible,* the Bible in Today's English Version. Old Testament: Copyright © American Bible Society, 1976; New Testament: Copyright © American Bible Society 1966, 1971, 1976. Used by permission.

Quotations marked KJV are from the King James Version of the Bible.

Dewey Decimal Classification: 241.5
Subject heading: FREEDOM

Library of Congress Catalog Card Number: 82-73932
Printed in the United States of America

For
Philip Brent Pollard
With love,
Dad

Preface

No world power has ever kept its freedom. Many have fought for and won freedom, but none have kept it for long.

It takes courage to win freedom. It takes character to keep it. Freedom does only one thing. It allows us to make choices. If we make the wrong choices, we lose our freedom.

God offers us a vision of national power. The word *vision* is not lightly chosen. There is a vast difference between dreams and visions. Dreamers recall wonderful events of the past and wish it could be like that again. People of vision look honestly at today and know, with leadership, it could be changed, and they begin to see that change! As they see it they activate it. With enough people like this, we can keep our freedom.

Contents

1   Keeping Free 11

2   Finding the Source of Freedom 18

3   The Freedom of Total Commitment 25

4   Keeping in Touch with Freedom's Source 31

5   Passing on the Gift of Freedom 37

6   Live and Help Live 43

7   The Freedom of Sexual Control 48

8   Don't Steal Freedom from Yourself 54

9   Loose Talk Sinks Freedom 59

10 Freedom Begins in Your Head 64

11 The Freedom to Go for It 70

12 Born Free! 76

13 Freedom Forever 82

14 How Your Freedom Was Won 89

15 Know the Ropes and You'll Be Free 96

16 Do You Think You're the Greatest? 103

17 Can You Read the Writing on the Wall? 109

18 Free Indeed! 116

1

Keeping Free

We lived a mile from the dirt road—really. Our house was one mile from the road maintained by the county. Terrapin Grade School was on that road. It was about the last rural school to be consolidated in Texas. By the time Miss Mueller came to be our teacher, the total student body numbered five: Albert, Freddy, Henry, Mary, and me. Mary was the prettiest girl in school!

We didn't have a lunchroom at Terrapin Grade School, so we all brought our lunches. We four boys usually had what was left over from breakfast—cold biscuits and sausage, ham, or bacon. Mary's lunch was different. Every day she had sandwiches made of store-bought sliced bread and bologna. I watched that girl eat those luscious lunches and dreamed of the day when I would grow up, make my fortune, and have all the sliced bread and bologna sandwiches I wanted.

Since Mary was the only girl in school, she was courted in grade-school fashion by all of us. Terrapin Grade School had a tall "teeter-totter," the biggest seesaw I ever saw. Once while Mary and I were seesawing, going way up and down, she said, "Frank, you're the one I like best." My, how that thrilled me! I almost burst a button off my overalls! But a minute later, when I was up, way up, she jumped off the other end and started talking to Albert. That almost broke my heart. I learned right then you can't trust a girl who is full of bologna!

11

Miss Mueller was the administration, faculty, and staff at Terrapin Grade School. She was principal, teacher, counselor, nurse, and janitor. And, she loved us. She noticed we were not living in the lap of luxury, so she taught us more than American history. She taught us about the American advantage. Injected into our thought stream was her contagious conviction: we can be just about anything we really want to be. Starting low in this land does not mean you have to stay low. Under the American advantage we are free to pursue our dreams.

That priceless issue is at stake in today's world conflict. Yet, irony of ironies, it is hardly mentioned. Our enemies don't think about it because they've never had it and can't conceive it. We don't think much about it because we've always had it and take it for granted. What is the most vital thing being risked in the uncertainties of our world? Freedom—the opportunity to make choices.

In Taiwan, my wife and I talked for an hour with a Red Chinese pilot who had defected from the mainland. He described a system of government which simply did not work: not enough food to eat or clothes to wear.

There is a lot of thinking space in a conversation when an interpreter is involved. The translator had just relayed our new friend's statements about government assigned houses and jobs. During the interim, when Chinese was spoken, I began to see it. The next translation came, telling of food stamps: "Only enough for two children, so you better not have three; only good in the place you are assigned to live, so you'd better stay put." The thrust of what he was saying hit like a heavyweight's left jab! He left the only people he had ever known, the only place he had ever lived, because he had no freedom to make choices.

This hard lesson was underlined when we returned to the US

and read in *Reader's Digest* a Russian defector's account. It was exactly the same story. No freedom. No choice. No life.

David Fite experienced the loss of freedom. Driving down a street in Havana, he heard the announcement on radio. In essence it informed him the car he was driving was no longer his. His home and everything in it now belonged to a nebulous thing called "The People."

He was tried and convicted for being an American spy. The case against him was simply the absence of a case against him. The prosecutor accused him of being so good a spy the authorities could find no convicting evidence. With that, David Fite was sentenced to die before a firing squad. For months he heard the executions outside his cell. Taunting guards kept promising he was next. Because so many in the world knew about his plight, the Castro officials finally decided to release him. David and his family were detained a bit longer because an inventory of the household goods they had bought, now property of "The People," showed a canister top missing. They had to give the officials their wedding rings, too, before they could leave.

Fite gave an example of indoctrination under the Castro regime. Six-year-old students were told to bow their heads and ask God for candy. At the conclusion of the prayer the teacher noted the absence of candy. Then the instruction was given to bow their heads, close their eyes, and ask Fidel Castro for candy. While they were doing this, a piece of candy was placed on each child's desk.

Many examples could be cited of those who do not enjoy the American advantage, the gift of freedom. A pertinent question for you and me is: Why do we have it? Why are we privileged with freedom when so many are denied it?

A large part of the answer is in our bloodstreams. We are descendants of people who got freedom and kept it for us.

Bixby of Boston lost five sons in one war. The sent her a letter. "I pray," he wrote, "your grief will be assuaged by good memories of those loved and lost and that you will feel some measure of pride in knowing you have laid upon the altar of freedom so costly a sacrifice." Many "costly sacrifices" have been laid upon the altar of freedom.

Marine Lieutenant Clebe McLeary lost both arms, an eye, an ear, and half his face in Vietnam. Twenty-four surgeries later his face was rebuilt. The men under his command gave him a plaque which states: "In this world of give and take, there are so few who are willing to give what it takes."

When the Japanese bombed Pearl Harbor, there were six boys in our home. Within weeks I was the only one. All of my brothers volunteered and served the full length of World War II. I was seven years old, and I will never forget how anxious they were to go. What I didn't realize was how young some of them were. On Eddie's seventeenth birthday he was part of the Marine landing force on Guadalcanal.

We moved to town shortly after the boys went to war. I got a paper route. Many of my customers had little blue flags with white stars hanging in their windows. The number of stars indicated how many in that family were in the service. Our family had the only five-star flag in town! We had to travel sixty miles to find one.

My favorite customers had only one star on their flag. They just had one child. Noticing I was about Boy Scout age they encouraged me to join the local troop. When I did, they gave me their son's uniform and Scout's manual. She always had ice tea on the hot days and hot chocolate on the cold days when I collected for the paper. He was my hero. A favorite spot for several boys was his office at the train depot where he worked as the Western Union telegraph operator. In widemouthed fascination we watched as he received and sent telegrams. One day he received one of those dreaded messages which began: "We regret to inform you." He had received and delivered those before, but this one was addressed to him and told of the death of his only son. Another costly sacrifice laid upon the altar of freedom.

At Gettysburg, Lincoln said: "The world will little note, nor long remember what we say here, but it can never forget what they did here. It is for us the living, rather, to be dedicated here to the unfinished work which they who fought here have thus far so nobly advanced."[1]

Freedom will forever be an "unfinished work." What is our part in this task? How do we keep free? Where is a nation's safeguard?

History, of course, only has negative answers. The little boy was right when on a test he wrote: "The only thing we learn from history is that we don't learn anything from history." History has shown us that a nation's safeguard is not in commerce or Tyre would never have fallen; not in art or Greece would never have fallen; not in religious ritualism or Jerusalem would never have fallen; not in political organization or Rome would never have fallen; and not in military might or Germany would never have fallen.

A country's safeguard is in its character. It takes courage to win freedom. It takes character to keep it. Freedom only does one thing—it gives us the opportunity to make choices. If we use our freedom to make wrong choices, we lose it. That's true individually and collectively.

Several years ago Dr. Kenneth McFarland led a group of experts who talked to people all over America. They went into large cities and small villages. General Motors had asked them to discover what Americans were really like in order to understand what kind of people would be buying cars. These experts fulfilled their assignment and then stayed longer in

conference. They had seen something which frightened them.
"This country is in danger," they said, "but the danger is not
from without. It is from within. The thing that could well
destroy us is not a bomb but an idea, the idea that we are no
longer morally responsible for our own conduct nor economically responsible for our own welfare."

Do you know that when Moses came down from that
mountain he was not a preacher with ten suggestions for those
who might opt to be religious? He was the leader of a brand-
new nation with ten principles for keeping free.

There is a positive preamble to the Ten Commandments. It
is found in Exodus 20:2, "I am the Lord your God, who
brought you out of the land of Egypt" (NASB). For the first
time in their lives these people were free. For hundreds of
years they had lived where the government told them to live,
worked where and how long the government ordered. For the
past generation the government had killed every male child
born to them. Now they were free.

The Lord said, "I made you free, right?"

They would have to answer, "Right!"

"So your God wants you to be free, right?"

"Right!"

"Now," he said, "let me tell you how to keep free." And he
gave them these ten principles for national and individual
survival.

People and nations do not break the Ten Commandments.
They only break themselves against them. We are morally
responsible for our own conduct. And all who can be must be
economically responsible for their own welfare. To the pseu-
dospiritual and lazy group in the church in Thessalonica, Paul
wrote: "For even when we were with you, we used to give you
this order: if anyone will not work, neither let him eat. For we
hear that some among you are leading an undisciplined life,

doing no work at all, but acting like busybodies. Now such persons we command and exhort in the Lord Jesus Christ to work in quiet fashion and eat their own bread" (2 Thess. 3:10-12, NASB).

I never realized what a great dad I had until he was gone. My father was what some people might call "handicapped." He was blind in one eye and his "good" eye was not very good. An arm had been mangled in a series of accidents, and it sort of hung at his side. He had a third-grade education, a wife, and seven boys. While I was growing up, he always seemed to have at least two jobs. I watched him leave the house before sunup and come home after sundown—week after week and year after year. Not once did he ask for any assistance. Never did he even suggest that our "better-off" neighbors owed us anything they had. He was never wealthy, never had much, but he was a great man. He was great because he was economically responsible. He worked, with quietness, and always ate his bread.

America has freedom now because it has a heritage of people who understood the responsibility of freedom—moral and economic responsibility. For all freedom does is give us the right to make choices. If we use our freedom to make wrong choices, we will lose it. We must never forget that freedom is not free.

---

[1]Henry Steele Commager, *Documents of American History* (New York: Appleton-Century-Croft Publishers, 1963), p. 429.

2

Finding the Source of Freedom

Exodus 20:1-6

What does it mean to you to be free? It may mean you and I can pursue our lifework. There are many countries in the world in which I would not be free to do what I do. Maybe that's true for you, too. It's good to be free to make choices, to make some decisions about our lives. Of course there's always the danger our choices can cause us to lose our freedom.

Freedom means much more than the opportunity to do what we like or go where we want. A lot of people do what they like but seldom like what they do. Some have all the goods of life, it seems, but no life. They have everything to live with but nothing to live for.

Handling freedom is like handling nitroglycerin. It may be a good feeling to have so much power in your hands, but you'd best be careful, or it will destroy you. Too many feed the hunger in their hearts—that appetite for living—with junk food, ways of living that destroy. The result is an unhealthy life-style which is anything but free.

What is freedom? To borrow a phrase from the US Army, it is the ability to "be all that you can be," to fulfill your potential while thoroughly enjoying the process.

Who among us hasn't said in our hearts . . . "I want to be free"?

Let's talk about how people and nations can be free—really

free. It must begin with understanding the source of freedom, with learning where freedom begins, where it comes from.

From God's Word hear Exodus 20:1-6 (NASB):

Then God spoke all these words, saying,

"I am the Lord your God, who brought you out of the land of Egypt, out of the house of slavery.

"You shall have no other gods before Me.

"You shall not make for yourself an idol, or any likeness of what is in heaven above or on the earth beneath or in the water under the earth.

"You shall not worship them or serve them; for I, the Lord your God, am a jealous God, visiting the iniquity of the fathers on the children, on the third and the fourth generations of those who hate Me, but showing lovingkindness to thousands, to those who love Me and keep My commandments (NASB).

If you want to be free to be all that you can be, these verses contain the most important truths you will ever confront. I am about to share with you the one fact on which freedom rests. If you don't get this, you'll never be free.

It's a truth which may be a little hard for you to swallow. So I beg you, if this thought doesn't suit your taste right away, please don't spit it out. At least let your mind chew on it for a while.

Here it is. You and I will be slaves to something or someone. We were created to be controlled. We were made to be mastered.

Freedom, then, comes by choosing the best master. The only freedom we have is to choose what controls us. Have you noticed how much freedom is lost in the name of freedom?

Someone says, "I am free to take a drink." Many times the drink takes the person.

"I am free to do drugs," you may say. Soon comes the sad

realization that you are not doing drugs, the drugs are doing you.

We can be slaves of work, idleness, love, lust, and ambition. You could continue this list, demonstrating how people are hurt or helped by whatever "magnificent obsession" claims them.

Here is the foundation upon which freedom is built, "I am the Lord your God" (v. 2, NASB). He is your Creator, your source of life. "In him," declares the Scripture, "we live, and move, and have our being" (Acts 17:28). The air we breathe and the beat of our hearts are in his hands. He is God. Resist that, and we destroy ourselves. Accept it, and we find freedom.

Freedom comes when we crown God as "number one" in our lives. That's why he commanded, "You shall have no other gods before Me" (Ex. 20:3, NASB).

Just as a truck is free to roll far and long if it stays on the highway, as a train is free and powerful unless it jumps the tracks, so are we free to enjoy God's gift of abundant life so long as we stay under the rule of God. That's the way we are made.

He must be number one. This position of priority calls for a synchronized commitment of life and lip, of walk and talk. High flights of worship on Sunday must be accompanied by straight and honest walking during the week.

One morning I was called by a congenial man, asking me to speak at a stockholder's banquet. This fellow, undoubtedly a sales leader, told me he had heard I was the best banquet speaker to be found, and his company wanted the best. My, how I wanted to go! But I couldn't. Wanting to help out I asked, "Have you heard of Zig Ziglar of Dallas?"

"Yes," he said, "we've already called him, and he can't make it either."

He told me I was number one, but really I was at best a distant second.

In my case that's something to smile about. But it is serious business to play that game with God. Sunday declarations that he is number one become sinful discrepancies when on Monday we relegate him to a distant second place behind profession, pleasure, or whatever.

"Seek ye first the kingdom of God, and his righteousness" (Matt. 6:33), and all you need for successful living is yours, promised our Lord Christ.

But what is meant when we say "God"? What kind of picture does the word *God* print in your mind? How do you know it's a true picture?

Life's supreme tragedy is not that you may not believe in God but that the idea you have of God may not be a true one.

It's important that we have in mind a clear picture of God. That's why he commanded, "Thou shalt not make unto thee any graven image" (v. 4). It means: "Don't reduce your idea of God to something smaller than he is."

We Americans often smile at the ignorant and primitive practice of making gods of wood or stone or metal. Yet we may be the most idolatrous of all. We like to create God in our minds. The Scripture states, "God created man in his own image" (Gen. 1:27), but our revised translation would honestly read: "And man created God to his own liking."

Have you heard this?

> I'm going to sit down and make myself
>   a God.
> I'll have a faith that won't make me
>   seem odd.
> I want this God available when it is
>   convenient.

Of course his doctrines will be ever so
   lenient.
I'm going to create my own God you see
Because I don't want my God embarrassing
   me.

AUTHOR UNKNOWN

Very real problems with this mental idolatry are recognized immediately. First, you have created a god who is as weak as you are. Problem number two: in judgment you will stand before God as he is and not as you have conveniently conjured up him.

Then how can we know him? How do we discover what God is really like?

He has answered that question. In fact, for thousands of years God has been revealing himself.

In Eden, he was there with Adam and Eve. What a perfect picture of happiness. But sin destroyed that bliss and the first couple were, by their own actions, banished from that fellowship.

God, in his love, did not give up on people. He didn't say, "You've blown it. You had your chance." No, he loves us. He wants to be with us. So he began a series of progressively showing himself. Gradually he revealed himself to people. Periodically, he spoke to the first fathers. In the ark of the covenant he dwelt among his people. Lovingly he spoke through the prophets. And then he came, in Christ!

In Eden it was God with people. In Moses' day it was God among his people. Through the prophets, God spoke to his people. But in Christ, God became a person.

Philip caused Christ to spell it out with unmistakable clarity when he said, "Lord, if you'll just show us the Father, we'll be satisfied." Our Lord replied, "Don't you know, Philip? Can't you see it? If you've seen me, you've seen the Father" (see John 14:9).

Two first-grade buddies were enjoying the recreation afforded by a backyard swing set. Presently, one said, "I had a good time in Vacation Bible School this morning. Why don't you go with me tomorrow?"

"What's Vacation Bible School?"

"We have it at church. We play games, sing, and learn about Jesus Christ."

"Who's Jesus Christ?"

In wisdom surely born of the spirit of God, the six-year-old answered, "Jesus Christ is the best picture of God that's ever been took." In fact, declares the Word of God, he is the only picture of God that's ever been taken.

Like millions of others, Saul of Tarsus discovered this one day and his life was never the same again. He was a religious man, but religion without Christ at its center is empty and evil. So he left the prestige, power, and wealth of his religious position to become a slave of Jesus Christ. He wrote of his Lord Christ, "in whom we have redemption, the forgiveness of sins. And He is the image of the invisible God" (Col. 1:14-15, NASB). "The visible likeness of the invisible God" (GNB)—the only picture of God that's ever been taken.

He is the only true picture of God you'll ever see. He is the only access to God you'll ever have. If you can't see God in Christ, you'll never see him. If you can't find God in Christ, you'll never find him. He came all the way from heaven to declare God's love for you, to pay for your sin debt, to offer you the shared victory of his empty tomb. Most of all he came to set you free. Jesus Christ is God on a mission of liberation. He came to set the prisoners free!

Is something in you saying, "I want to be free"? Then join the crowd of truly liberated people shouting, Christ set me free.

In one line the Bible describes what you may be feeling about your life: "Wretched man that I am! Who will set me free from the body of this death?" (Rom. 7:24, NASB).

The next line declares the freedom available to you: "Thanks be to God through Jesus Christ our Lord!" (v. 25, NASB).

Several years ago I heard a story I'll never forget. I've read a lot and looked a lot of places, trying to document the tale, but haven't been able to do so. So I don't know if the story is true. In a minute I think you'll understand what I mean when I say it's one of those tales that's true whether it happened or not.

Some years back a man bought an old Model T Ford. On a lonely stretch of road the old Ford just stopped running; it died. The stranded motorist was bewildered. He didn't even know how to unlatch the hood. Presently an apparently wealthy man stopped his car, got out, and offered assistance. Soon he had uncovered the engine, made an adjustment on the old carburetor, and set the spark lever on the steering wheel. With one turn of the hand crank the old Model T Ford ran like the day it was made. The grateful owner extended his hand and said, "Mister, I want to thank you, but I don't even know your name."

"You're very welcome," he replied. "My name is Henry Ford."

You see, Henry Ford knew how to make a Model T run because he made it. God knows what it takes to make your life run smoothly because he made you. Find Christ, and you'll find the source of your freedom.

3

The Freedom of Total Commitment

Exodus 20:7

In preceding pages we've been talking about freedom, where we get it, and once we've gotten it how to keep it. We must keep reminding ourselves that, while it takes courage to win freedom, it takes character to keep it. Posted in a prominent place on the wall of our awareness we should keep this truth: all freedom does is give us the opportunity to make choices. If we use our freedom to make the wrong choices or to make no choices, then we lose it.

Today's principle for keeping free calls us to a truth seen in the lives of people all around us. Who are the really strong people? Who are those who seem to know how to live life at its fullest? They are people of purpose, people who have discovered the freedom of total involvement.

Here, my friend, I must warn you of a tricky danger. It is true that any time you aim your efforts in one direction and commit yourself to one purpose, you will be strong. You will probably succeed. You will most likely climb to the top of any ladder you choose. But if you choose the wrong purpose, the success you achieve will lead to ultimate failure. It's a sad thing to climb to the top of a ladder and learn you've leaned it against the wrong wall. After all the struggle, you find something entirely different than you expected.

Because of that danger God, who made you, knows you,

and loves you, lays out this principle for keeping free: "Thou shalt not take the name of the Lord thy God in vain" (Ex. 20:7).

What does that mean?

Our first thoughts suggest this to be a prohibition against cursing and profanity. And it is. God is very serious about his name. He knows that the way we use his name reflects how we really feel about him. "Hallowed be thy name" (Matt. 6:9) is the prayer of every serious Christian. One of the symptoms of a seriously sick society is national irreverence. America, as a whole, is acting like an undisciplined adolescent, laughing at and crudely trampling on values our forefathers thought holy while ignoring the sure signs of coming judgment.

Yet there is much more in this commandment than a warning from God not to curse. The word *vain* means "empty, lifeless, lacking a sense of urgency." This is a call to repent of the sin of mild religion. Taking God's name in vain means you do not have a sense of urgency about him. Perhaps the greatest sinning with the name of God is not done in barrooms where his holy name is interspersed with sewer talk, but in churches where the words of songs, prayers, and sermons are not really meant.

We take God's name in vain when we claim faith in God but refuse to get excited about it. Declaring love for him we don't really intend to live out is taking his name in vain.

One man said: "When I was a child, we got up early on Sunday morning, did the necessary farm chores, dressed in our best clothes, hitched the horses to the wagon, and drove for an hour to get to church. There we joyously thanked God for his provision, committed our lives to him, and sang from our souls, 'We'll work till Jesus comes.'" Now we sleep late, drive in an air-conditioned car for ten minutes, sit in cushioned comfort, listening to a paid choir sing, "Art thou weary, art thou languid?" The sin of mild, lifeless religion is a serious matter.

We take God's name in vain if we say we are Christians but don't care if the world goes to hell.

We take his name in vain when we call him "Lord" and do not offer ourselves to him.

We are guilty of empty, mild religion when we profess belief in Christ, but it makes no difference in how we live.

When we take his name but without conviction and urgency, then our profession is cheap, easy, empty, and vain.

The broad gap between what we are and what we ought to be is often noted by the world around us. Viewing the often obvious difference between our profession and our performance, one man said, "They're praising God on Sunday, but they'll be all right on Monday. It's just a little habit they've acquired."

Some years ago a best-selling novel began, "The courthouse clock struck twelve and the church on the corner was giving up its dead." You and I know the church of our Lord Christ has many critics. I tried to share Christ with one such man. He is one of those people who has been educated far beyond his intelligence. To him sophistication is a sneer. He has nothing to offer but offense. He contributes nothing but criticism. He can hardly wait to tell me the latest church joke.

"Know the newest definition of a hypocrite? It's a teenage boy, sitting in church, holding the hand of the prettiest girl in school while singing, 'All that thrills my soul is Jesus.'"

To me that story was distasteful, but it represents a condition in the church which is distastefully true.

The disparity between saying and doing is the church's heaviest drag. And all seekers of victorious living need to

understand that this disparity is what causes life to be a drag
for you. While the sin of mild, anemic religion dishonors him,
it weakens us and destroys life.

The besetting sin of this age is boredom. Boredom comes
from a lust for leisure, a life without responsibility, without
challenge, with no consuming purpose.

How well Shakespeare's Macbeth expressed it:

> To-morrow, and to-morrow, and to-morrow,
> Creeps on this petty pace from day to day
> To the last syllable of recorded time;
> And all our yesterdays have lighted fools
> The way to dusty death. Out, out, brief
>   candle!
> Life's but a walking shadow, a poor player
> That struts and frets his hour upon the stage
> And then is heard no more: it is a tale
> Told by an idiot, full of sound and fury,
> Signifying nothing.

There's no joy in empty living. Joy and victory are found in
commitment. Look around you. Who do you know who is
really free? Who seeks to have a zest for life and power for
living? It is probably someone who is committed to something
or someone outside themselves. When that commitment is to
the Author of life and freedom, you are really free.

The lifeless, unhappy Christian of today is characterized by
inturning eyeballs and itching palms. He judges his spiritual
experience by what he got out of it rather than what he put into
it. He is constantly taking his spiritual pulse. He asks
questions like, "How do I feel? Am I having a good time?
How spiritual am I?"

Contrast that with the example and challenge of our Lord
Christ. Life radiated from him. He was full of life. So evident
it was that people kept asking him how to have life. What was

his answer? "Whoever tries to gain his own life will lose it; but whoever loses his life for my sake will gain it" (Matt. 10:39, GNB). Real life is found in giving it away. The Bible talks about taking up your cross and following Christ (v. 38). The cross for Christ was God's will for him. The "cross" for you and me is God's will for our lives. He promises, "Find God's will for you daily, follow that, and you will live!"

Now let's think about some of the people who heard him say that and did it. How about Simon Peter? Have you wondered what Simon Peter's life would have been like if he had not decided to give total commitment to Jesus Christ? Of course we don't know. We would never have heard of him. No one would have heard of him except a few people around the Sea of Galilee. He would have spent his life committed to the task of catching and selling a few fish each day. The small commitment means a small life, without zest and power. Now I am convinced that if our Lord's will for Peter had been that he stay in the fishing business, his life still would have been large and full. He would have been fishing for the glory of Christ, and that makes the difference in two worlds.

I heard about a tombstone in Scotland which read something like this: "Here lies the bones of Donald Graham who cobbled shoes for forty years to the glory of God!" An epitaph of a life well done.

What about Paul, the apostle? When he became a follower of Christ, he was already a big shot, a success. He was ambitious, driving, ever climbing the ladder of success. In Philippians 3:8, he declared that the life he had in Christ made all the things he once lived for look like garbage.

Hear his conviction about how life is to be lived:

Brethren, I do not regard myself as having laid hold of it yet; but one thing I do: forgetting what lies behind and reaching forward to what lies ahead,

I press on toward the goal for the prize of the upward call of God in Christ Jesus (Phil. 3:13-14, NASB).

"This one thing I do," not all these things I dabble in. If the one thing your life is centered upon is the world's greatest cause; if it is linked to the God of creation, salvation, and judgment; if the compelling desire of your life leads ultimately to hearing him say, "Well done, good and faithful servant" (Matt. 25:23)—then, my friend, you are free to live!

A missionary said, "Very few people know what it means to commit their lives totally to God. I think I do, and I feel sorry for those who don't."

"Thou shalt not take the name of the Lord thy God in vain" (Ex. 20:7). Sound negative? Not on your life! It is one solid section in the foundation of real freedom. God is simply saying, "Practice what you profess, and you will know the freedom of total commitment."

4

Keeping in Touch with Freedom's Source

Exodus 20:8-11

Life's best things are often lost by neglect. This is especially true of the power, love, and freedom of a Christian. Many of us would join the poet William Cowper in lamenting:

> Where is the blessedness I knew
> When first I saw the Lord?
> Where is the soul-refreshing view
> Of Jesus and His Word?
>
> What precious hours I once enjoyed,
> How sweet their memories still;
> But they left an aching void
> This world can never fill.

It's true, isn't it, that often we lose what we treasure by taking it for granted and neglecting it. The weeping husband confessed, "I took her for granted. I never told her or showed her how much I love her." The crushed parent wishes for the impossible opportunity to go back ten years and start over again with a rebellious child. The carnal Christian, caught in the devil's yo-yo—knowing right, doing wrong, repenting one day, returning to sin the next—yearns for the sweet peace and moral power of his early Christian days. In addition to a daily spiritual maintenance program, God's Word declares a most needed ingredient for keeping our freedom:

Remember the sabbath day, to keep it holy. Six days you shall
labor and do all your work, but the seventh day is a sabbath of the
Lord your God; in it you shall not do any work, you or your son or
your daughter, your male or your female servant or your cattle or
your sojourner who stays with you. For in six days the Lord made the
heavens and the earth, the sea and all that is in them, and rested on
the seventh day; therefore the Lord blessed the sabbath day and made
it holy (Ex. 20:8-11, NASB).

A large part of keeping free is to set aside a day to remember
who we are. We must not let the hassle of making a living keep
us from having life. Our Lord God commands there be a day
set aside to remember and to teach others to remember and
honor the One who is our source of life, breath, and all
things—including our freedom.

In setting aside one day out of seven to pay honor to our
Lord God we shall be helping others do the same. On almost
every other page of God's Word is the declaration of our
responsibility for the impact of our lives on other people. We
must not ignore this. Our daily living will either hurt or help,
lift up or pull down others around us. The increasingly unusual
sight of a family cleaned, shined, and on their way to church
has an enormous effect. People working in yards, preparing
their boats, or engaged in a bleary-eyed search for the morning
paper will take note. A college student, in September, was the
only one in his dorm to get up on Sunday morning and attend
Sunday School and church. By October four others had joined
him. "You didn't say anything to us," they explained, "but
your actions reminded us that this is the Lord's Day."

Even more critical is the influence factor when you shift it
from the neighborhood into your own home. Children are
quick to pick up on priorities. You don't have to tell them what
matters most to you, they quickly see it. They get the message
when weekday commitment to work or school is nonnegotia-

ble while worshiping God is the lesser of many options for the weekend. How inconsistently do parents who insist on proper health habits and education for their children either let them starve spiritually, or permissively allow them to swallow any diet of spiritual junk food they may choose.

Remembering and observing the Lord's Day is important to others, and it is important to us. We need it. Without it we lose our grasp on his freedom.

And it isn't enough to rush in and out of one service, having sort of tipped our hat to God in the process.

Once a church which considered itself to be the most prestigious church in a suburban community which considers itself to be the most prestigious city in our state talked to me about being their pastor. Some of the shining glitter of that possibility was dimmed when the deacon chairman informed me he never made it to church on Sunday evening because his Sunday afternoon golf game left him exhausted. Noting my startled reaction he presented a noble defense of his view of observing the Lord's Day. I wasn't as impressed by his argument as he was. Actually, what he said was underwhelming.

Yet, he represents thousands of people who consider themselves Christians. They are victims of what has been called the "Angelic Fallacy." It means we think ourselves to be angels instead of sinful people in need of God's grace. It is the sin of a supposed spiritual superiority which has outgrown the need of weekly observance of the Lord's Day. The self-proclaimed angel has gone higher and no longer needs the support of the church. He thinks he has graduated when actually he is nothing more than a dropout, leaning to his own understanding. Instead of God's wisdom, he honestly professes to be proud of his sin when he should be ashamed.

The liberated Hebrews wanted to worship God in their way

instead of his. They made and worshiped a golden, baby bull
(Ex. 32). Please think it no impropriety to remind you that
many considering themselves to be liberated Christians have
focused their Lord's Day activities around a lot of baby bull.
God always calls us to worship on his terms, not ours. His
reaction to whatever shape our golden calf takes is consistently
severe.

The angelic fallacy is probably the most damaging sin of
modern Christendom. It blinds us to our sinful weakness and
leads us to a spiritually defeating self-confidence.

My favorite newspaper reading is the column of Roddy
Stinson. One day I carelessly put a quarter in the wrong
machine and soon found myself reading another writer's daily
offering. This journalist was decrying the fact that a murderer
had professed faith in Christ and declared he had been saved.
She said she didn't like the word *saved*. She prefers the term
enlightened. Ah, the angelic fallacy. We don't need to be
saved. We only need to be enlightened. To be saved means you
know you are hopelessly lost. To be enlightened only calls for
a little instruction.

Jesus never said, "I have come to teach and enlighten those
who are confused." He did say, "I have come to seek and to
save those who are lost" (see Luke 19:10).

Nicodemus wanted to be enlightened. John 3 tells us he was
as good a man as the institutional religion of that day could
turn out. He was respected, religious, and rich. Yet he didn't
have life. Not like Jesus had it. So he came seeking some new
insight, some new thought, some enlightenment. Our Lord
Christ said, "Nicodemus, you'll never find what you're
searching for in your own mind, for you are a sinful creature.
You must be born from above. Your salvation is not in your
head but in your commitment to the one who will pay the
supreme price for your sins." In John 3:17, Jesus told

Nicodemus he had not come to judge the world; our sins have already done that. Jesus declared that he was sent to save the world.

We must become serious about observing the Lord's Day because the world needs that salvation. We must set a priority on this day because we are sinful creatures in need of the support afforded by worshiping God and fellowshipping with other Christians.

Paul Elmer More, a distinguished philosopher, wrote:

I am impressed by the weakness of men and their dependence on help; I see my own humiliating limitations. . . . To fall on our knees and supplicate for pardon and help seems to me not an abdication of our manhood, but an acknowledgement of our sin, an act of wisdom and enlightened will.[1]

There is no doubting God's seriousness about his day. We may call it trivial, but it is important to God. This is the longest of all the commandments. God knows we need the day because without it we will lose sight of who we are. In Mark 2:27 our Lord asserted, "The Sabbath was made for man, and not man for the Sabbath." This day is for us. We need it, for without it we lose the dynamic of our freedom in Christ.

The Bible refers to the northern tribes of Israel which did not survive the captivity. Sometimes they are called the "ten lost tribes of Israel." What does it mean by saying they were lost? They were not lost in migration. It was not a geographical loss. Everyone knew where they were. They lost their identity. They were the people of God, called to be a blessing to the world. But they lost that. They simply became like the world around them, so they were lost to the purpose to which God saved them and called them.

The Southern Kingdom survived and still exists. Why? Because in captivity they formed synagogues. They came together weekly and worshiped the Lord God and constantly reminded themselves of their purpose and calling.

God has many "lost tribes" today. They are not lost geographically. Their names are still on church rolls. They have lost their identity as people of God. They have become like the world around them. They are enslaved by the same habits, greed, fears, and anxieties as those without God. They have not kept in touch with the source of their freedom, and they lost it.

Roy McClain told of how relatives at the hearing were shocked to learn that an infidel farmer had willed all of his property to the devil. There was no doubting the validity of the will. The problem was, how do you give a farm to the devil? It was finally decided. Nothing would be done with the property. No one would till the soil, service the machinery, or maintain the buildings. Soon eroding fields, rusting machinery, and rotting, unpainted buildings were proof that his wishes had been fulfilled. The farm had gone to the devil by default.

The freedom to live as God's happy children is lost in like manner. To prevent this tragic loss we must set aside a day each week, dedicated to God, to fellowship with his people and to his kingdom task. In this way we keep in touch with the source of our freedom.

Often we hear people say, "TGIF—thank goodness it's Friday!" What an enormous impact in individual lives and in our world could be accomplished if we could hear each week from God's people a resounding "PGIS—Praise God it's Sunday!"

---

1. Paul Elmer More, *Pages from an Oxford Diary* (Princeton, NJ: Princeton University Press, 1937), p. xxv.

5

Passing on the Gift of Freedom

Exodus 20:12

I hope you will forever engrave on the wall of your awareness this foundation fact concerning the Ten Commandments: they are God-given principles for keeping free. Never entertain the shallow notion that Moses was a preacher with ten suggestions for people who might want to be religious. He was the leader of a brand-new nation of people who were free for the first time in their lives. In the very positive preamble to the Ten Commandments, God said, "I made you free. I want you to be free. Now here are ten principles which must be obeyed if you are to keep on being free."

Let's look at Exodus 20:12 and read together one of those principles for keeping free: "Honor your father and your mother, that your days may be prolonged in the land which the Lord your God gives you."

John Drakeford has rightly stated, "The home is a laboratory for living." How true that is. If we learn to live well at home, we can live well in the world. If we can produce the kind of people who know how to honor their fathers and mothers, we will have the kind of people who can live long "in the land," that is, who can keep the freedom God has given us.

Most of us who have reared children feel tinges of guilt when we confront this Scripture. Being a parent, in our society, is one of life's most challenging jobs. Few of us feel we have done it well.

I heard of a preacher who, in his young years, had a sermon titled "How to Raise Children." After children were born into his family, he changed the title of his sermon to "Suggestions on How to Raise Children." When those children became teenagers, he changed the title again. Now it is called "Helpful Hints for Fellow Strugglers."

It needs to be noted that sometimes parents can do a good job and have a child to fail. In Judges 13—16 is found the intriguing story of a man named Samson. God had great plans for Samson. He was born of dedicated, God-fearing parents. In Judges 13:8 we read of Samson's father, Manoah, praying for God's guidance in the rearing of this child. Samson, you recall, was very strong. He had muscles in places where most of us don't even have places. He was the original "Incredible Hulk." With his long hair and bulging body he may have looked like one of the iron pumpers from Muscle Beach, California.

In spite of the blessings of God and the example and teaching of his parents, Samson rejected their values and advice. He practiced limitless sex, gave in to many other undisciplined desires, and habitually destroyed anything or anyone who got in his way.

Yes, sometimes parents can do their best and have a child turn away from their values. It's also possible for parents to do a bad job and have a child to succeed.

Jonathan, the close friend of David, was an Old Testament example of the generation gap going in the opposite direction. Jonathan had ideas and values which were vastly superior to those of his father, King Saul.

Most of the time, however, children will follow the patterns of what they learn at home. In 2 Timothy 1:5, Paul wrote to Timothy, "I am mindful of the sincere faith within you, which first dwelt in your grandmother Lois, and your mother Eunice, and I am sure that it is in you as well." Timothy was led to a solid faith through the witness and example of consistent Christian living by his mother and grandmother.

However, when the witness is not consistent, when children see their parents living one way in public and another in private, then the effects can be disastrous.

The Book of 2 Samuel records the doings of a young man who could have been a patron saint for latter-day hippies, long hair and all! His name was Absalom. He was severely disappointed by the disparity between his father's ideals and actions. David's sex partnership with another man's wife and his success in disposing of her husband probably triggered Absalom's bitter rebellion.

In a cell on death row I found a tall young man who couldn't have been more than twenty years old. He had been found guilty of killing another human being; in fact, he admitted to killing several people. He was the son of a gangster whose bullet-riddled body had been found in the trunk of his car just months before. The young man had been raised to be a criminal. He said, "My dad told me I had the right to take anything or anyone I was smart enough or tough enough to take." He had followed the pattern of what he had learned at home. As I looked into his bright blue eyes I wondered how different he would have been if his father had been different. Behind this command for children to honor their father and mother is the call of God for fathers and mothers to be honorable.

This commandment has a great deal to do with national survival. If we are to live together agreeably and peacefully, our young must learn to have a healthy respect for authority. Their first authority figures are their parents. A child will not be educated unless he respects his teachers. His first teachers are his parents. He must learn to stop at the red light even when he doesn't want to. If he doesn't learn that, he may kill himself and some others, too. His first traffic lights are his father and mother. When he gets a job, he must be able to take and follow instructions from his supervisor. His first supervisors are his parents. The home is a laboratory for living. We establish our patterns there.

Those taught to honor their fathers and mothers are most likely to do the best. If we learn to live well at home, we can probably live well in the world.

You see, the power to be free lies not in who you know or what you have but who you are. Freedom, individually, means character. Freedom, collectively, for a nation means enough people have the character vital to keeping free. Genesis 18:32 declares that the presence of ten good people would have prevented the destruction of Sodom and Gomorrah. Second Kings 18 records an attack of the Assyrians on Jerusalem. Three representatives of King Hezekiah were sent to talk to the commander of the Assyrian troops (v. 18). They were just outside the walls of Jerusalem. In fact, some of the people of Jerusalem were on the wall listening to their conversation. The Assyrian commander told King Hezekiah's officers that he knew the king was counting on an arms agreement he made with Egypt. "Why, I imagine he's straining his eyes to the east now," he said, "looking for the cloud of dust which means the king of Egypt has come through. The horses are on their way." In verse 23 we read, "Now therefore, come, make a bargain with my master the king of Assyria, and I will give you two thousand horses, if you are able on your part to set riders on them." That's the problem with horses or tanks or planes. You have to have men to ride them. If you don't have strong people, you don't have what it takes to keep free.

China thought they could protect themselves with the Great

Wall. "No one can take us, we have the Wall," they reasoned. Yet each time the enemy attacked they bribed the gatekeepers and marched right through the Wall. If you don't have strong people, you can't be strong.

Strong people are developed in strong homes. People who learn to give honor and respect to fathers and mothers are the people who become honorable and respected.

I heard Ken McFarland tell about a family who lived on the plains of Kansas. It was during a time when the kids entered the social set by eating at the big table with the grown-ups when several families gathered about once a quarter. It would take a half day to drive to the meeting place, and this was the only social life they had. After their thirteenth birthday, the children got to come and sit at the table with the grown-ups. Now, the parents were judged by how their child acted at that meal. The man telling the story said, "It was my time. I just had my thirteenth birthday. My mother coached me and told me how to sit and act—how to do all of these things. I worked at that. I didn't want to embarrass my parents. That night I was very nervous. After a while everything seemed to be going all right. I was doing OK. People began to smile and look at my parents and nod their heads. My folks were proud. I was feeling good. Then we came to the dessert. It was some plums floating around in juice. I really didn't know what to do; but I took a spoon, and that seemed to be all right—everybody nodded. I was eating that dessert and realized after a while I had something in my mouth that wasn't a plum. I rolled it around on the end of my tongue, and I knew it wasn't a plum because it had hair on it." Then somebody asked, "What did you do?" "I just swallowed the silly thing for the folks' sake." Now there has to come a time when people who are maturing are going to swallow some silly things for the folks' sake.

There's a poem that goes with that story:

> My son came home and he said to me,
>   "Today I saw a boy fall out of a tree.
> He couldn't get up from where he lay
>   and an ambulance came and took him away."
> I said to my son, "You saw the boy lying
>   pale in the dirt, but how many would you
>   say got hurt?"
> "Oh," said my son, "just the boy, no more.
> The crowd went away and all was the same
>   as before."
> "Oh, no, my son, not all was the same.
>   Just think of the family that bears that
>   boy's name.
> His father was hurt. His mother was hurt.
>   His sister was hurt, too.
> Right now, all those who love him are heart-
>   sick and blue.
> Remember, my son, you are part of a home.
>   Your joys and your sorrows are not yours
>   alone.
> So think straight, live straight, be kind
>   and be true; if for no other reason than
>   others love you."
>
>   AUTHOR UNKNOWN

If we produce people who can swallow some silly things for the folks' sake; if we can turn out the kind of child who thinks straight, lives straight, and is kind and true because they don't want to tarnish the name of God or their family, then we will be free for a long time!

"Honor your father and your mother, that your days may be prolonged in the land which the Lord your God gives you" (NASB).

6

Live and Help Live

Exodus 20:13

If I were to ask you, "What is the number one problem in your business, your home, and your neighborhood?" you would probably answer, "Human relations." Getting along with each other, functioning side by side, day by day, is one of life's great challenges.

You are well acquainted with the fact that all of the civilizations which have fallen, fell in on themselves. They were not beaten down from the outside. No civilization has ever been defeated from without. They have all died of internal complications. None of the estimated nineteen civilizations which have fallen were murdered, all committed suicide. The autopsies are monotonously repetitious. Each civilization has come into history's garbage dump because its people could not live together without destroying each other.

In the first section of the Ten Commandments we are told that keeping free means recognizing the supreme worth of God. Now we begin the last Five Commandments which declare the supreme worth of people made in God's image. Getting along with those people is a must if freedom is to be maintained. One sage said, "To dwell there above with the saints that we love, that will be glory! To dwell here below, with the saints we know, that's another story." Yet, we must dwell here below with others. How well we can do that determines our destiny.

43

The first principle for living together is: "Thou shalt not kill" (Ex. 20:13). May it be quickly said—this statement has nothing to do with capital punishment or warfare. Other Scriptures in the Levitical laws deal directly with those problems. This is not a cheap, one-shot answer to abortion or euthanasia. Each of these painful situations has to be worked out individually, praying for God's wisdom and applying the principles of love and sanctity for life.

Bible scholars agree this is a prohibition of murder. The Hebrew verb implies "violent and unauthorized killing." There is a vast difference between murder and killing. If this commandment were to be taken as a blanket prohibition of killing, then it would be wrong to kill insects, snakes, dangerous beasts, and rabid dogs. A vegetarian may say, "I don't believe in killing animals, so he pulls up vegetables— killing them by separating them from their source of life. You remember the example of Dr. Albert Schweitzer who built a great mission hospital in Lambaréné, Africa. He strictly forbade the killing of even so much as a fly or mosquito. Yet the good doctor and his associates were there in part to save lives by destroying the life of disease-bearing organisms and microbiological beings.

More is intended here than a prohibition against taking life. It is an encouragement to help each other save life. We see this clearly when our Lord interprets the Sixth Commandment:

You have heard that the ancients were told, "You shall not commit murder," and "Whoever commits murder shall be liable to the court."

But I say to you that every one who is angry with his brother shall be guilty before the court; and whoever shall say to his brother, "Raca," shall be guilty before the supreme court; and whoever shall say, "You fool," shall be guilty enough to go into the hell of fire.

If therefore you are presenting your offering at the altar, and there remember that your brother has something against you, leave your offering there before the altar, and go your way; first be reconciled to your brother, and then come and present your offering (Matt. 5:21-24, NASB).

Now there's a hard-hitting truth which, if caught cleanly, will blister more than your hands. In the mind of God, murder is more than an act. It is an attitude. You face the judgment of God when you allow hateful anger to cloud your relationship with another. You stand accountable for a severe sin if you ever hold contempt in your heart against any person. "Raca" was a sound more than a word. It was a clearing of the throat as though to say, "I spit on you." To call another person a "worthless fool" is to invite for yourself the fires of hell warned our Lord. Verses 24 and 25 state that there is no way you can worship God if ill feeling exists between you and another. First John 2:9 declares, "Anyone who claims to be in the light but hates his brother is still in the darkness" (NIV). Colossians 3:8 commands us to put aside anger, wrath, malice, and filthy communication.

You see, there is a positive side of this commandment. It does not mean that we are only to live and let live, but we are also to live and help live. When God walked this earth as a man, he was our example of compassion for the needs of all others. Not only did he condemn a murderer but also the ones who walked by without helping a wounded brother. The foundation of this commandment is that God values every person as much as he values me. This rule of living means that we see everyone as he does.

A lighting expert was given the job of illuminating a statue of a boy. First, he put the lights on the floor shining upon the boy's face. He stepped back and looked at it and was shocked—it made the boy look demented. He changed the lights. He tried every arrangement. Finally, he put the lights up above where they shone down on the boy's face. Then he stood back and smiled, for the boy looked like an angel.

There is truth for us in that story. When we look at people from the earthly level some look inferior, and it is easy to feel that "those people do not matter." But when we look at a person, any person, through the eyes of Christ with the light streaming down on him from God, then that life becomes sacred. Then you say, "I must not only let him live, I must help him live!"

Now we begin to see the great wisdom of our Lord's summation of the Commandments, "Love the Lord your God," and "Love your neighbor as yourself" (Matt. 22: 37,39, NIV).

Perhaps we don't pay enough attention to the last phrase of that statement: "as yourself." This commandment is asserting that neither by act nor attitude are you to take your own life. It is true that suicide is forbidden by God. We did not create our lives, and we don't have the right to take them. The very fact of life carries with it an obligation to live. We must leave in God's hands how he judges this violation of his law. He is love, and he knows all the circumstances and mental conditions and responsibility.

I heard about a man who decided to take his life. He was determined there would be no slipup. He took a small boat into a deep river. He tied a rope to an overhanging limb. He doused himself with gasoline. He had a loaded pistol in his hand. He put the noose around his neck and kicked the boat out from under his feet. At the same time he set himself afire and pulled the trigger on the pistol. Well, he missed his head and shot the rope in two. He fell in the water, putting out the fire. Later on he said, "If I hadn't known how to swim, I would have drowned!"

There are more ways to commit suicide than by taking your

physical life. You can have a wrong attitude toward yourself. By forgetting that you are a special, unique creation of God you can kill your potential. Just as hatred of others is a serious sin so is hatred of self. It is to the best interest of everyone that you be a happy, productive person, enjoying to the fullest all God made you to be.

I think this principle is God saying to us, "You can keep your freedom by living and helping others to live." In any society what really counts is the people. Edwin Markham was right:

> We are all blind, until we see
> That in the human plan,
> Nothing is worth the making if
> It does not make the man.
>
> Why build these cities glorious
> If man unbuilded goes?
> In vain we build the work, unless
> The builder also grows.

A critical mistake is to assume you have the right to more freedom than your neighbor. In protecting your neighbor's freedom, you protect your own. In helping your neighbor, you are helping yourself. Freedom is maintained as we live and help live.

7

The Freedom of Sexual Control

Exodus 20:14

We have to keep reminding ourselves the Ten Commandments are principles for maintaining freedom. They come directly from the One who created life, who intends us to have an abundant life (John 10:10). Freedom is one of the Bible's favorite synonyms for salvation. In John 8:36 our Lord Christ said of himself, "If the Son sets you free, then you will be really free" (GNB). Galatians 5:1 declares, "Freedom is what we have—Christ has set us free! Stand, then, as free people, and do not allow yourselves to become slaves again" (GNB).

Be aware, and that keenly, it is in the name of freedom, not restraint, that God commands, "You shall not commit adultery" (Ex. 20:14, NASB).

The sixth plank in freedom's platform is "Thou shalt not kill" (Ex. 20:13). Your freedom to live is dependent upon others' freedom to live. A free society works to make sure everyone has the right and freedom to live. This seventh principle for keeping free rests upon the same foundation—the fact that people, all people, are sacred. Each of us is made in the image of God. We must not violate the sacredness of another's personality. We don't toy or tamper with the affections of other people.

You and I are interested in what God's Word has to say about any subject. We believe the Bible is his Word for us. One biblical truth is clear to all who read it: God takes sexual sin seriously. Exodus 20:14 commands, "Thou shalt not commit adultery."

Surely you know that the wicked will not possess God's Kingdom. Do not fool yourselves; people who are immoral or who worship idols or are adulterers or homosexual perverts or who steal or are greedy or are drunkards or who slander others or are thieves—none of these will possess God's Kingdom (1 Cor. 6:9-10, GNB).

Revelation 21:8 calls the roll of unredeemed people destined for hell, "But cowards, traitors, perverts, murderers, the immoral, those who practice magic, those who worship idols, and all liars—the place for them is the lake burning with fire and sulfur, which is the second death" (GNB).

Listen to this straightforward language from Deuteronomy, "If a man is caught having intercourse with another man's wife, both of them are to be put to death. In this way you will get rid of this evil" (22:22, GNB).

Why so strong a prohibition of that which is so common in our society? Because adultery is a destroyer of freedom. A major crack causing the eventual crumbling and fall of every nation in history's garbage dump is this one.

What, then, do we do? How does one handle this fire burning within? How can we keep sexual passions from destroying us?

God's first word to us in this matter is *control*. The Bible declares that the fruit or result of being filled with the Spirit of God is self-control (Gal. 5:23). Who really is free—the one who gives in to every desire entering the mind or the one who is strong enough not to have to give in to every urge which comes along?

Little Johnny was sitting on a fence, looking at his neighbor's apple tree. His neighbor asked, "Johnny, are you trying to steal one of my apples?"

"No sir, I'm trying not to!"

Being free means being in control of yourself.

In the name of freedom the compulsive eater may gobble down every bit of food in sight. But the person really free is the one who doesn't have to have a cookie every time the thought occurs.

A distorted idea of freedom may assure the alcoholic he is free to take a drink whenever he feels like it. The man is really free if he doesn't have to take a drink when he feels like it.

Freedom doesn't mean doing anything you want to. Freedom means you have the ability to do what you ought to. You are in control.

Perhaps the hardest to tame of all the wild horses of instincts stampeding within us is called "lust." Thousands of years ago God prompted Jeremiah to pen a line which could fit well in an editorial page of today's newspapers: "They were like well-fed stallions wild with desire, each lusting for his neighbor's wife" (Jer. 5:8, GNB).

What do we do with this most animal of our instincts? Through the years three philosophies have dominated people's thinking. Each generation tries to convince itself the idea is new, but it's really just an ancient idea dressed in today's fashion. Interestingly enough, each way of living presents itself as freedom.

The first could be called "freedom from restraint." It is the opposite of control. What do you do with the wild horse? Let him run wild. Throw off restraint. "If it feels good, do it." This kind of "freedom" has been making slaves of people and nations for centuries.

Another approach could be called "freedom from desire." What do you do with the wild horse of passion? Kill it. This is the way of Buddha or Hinduism. Destroy feeling, become nothing, numb, and empty. I know a girl who jokingly said when her leg was hurting, "I wish I could just cut it off." This way of looking at life declares we should cut off all desire. It's like chopping off your head to stop a headache.

The third approach is the Christian way. We can call it "freedom of control." Don't kill the horse. Don't let it run wild. Tame it. Bridle it. Enjoy it because you have it under control.

Sex is the gift of God. He made us sexual creatures, but we are more. We are also social and spiritual creatures. A Christian shouldn't take to life like a dog takes to an alley. A Christian shouldn't use people like a "No Deposit, No Return" soft-drink bottle, either drinking them dry and throwing them away or setting them aside when there is a yen for a different taste. We shouldn't play that deceitful game saying "I love you" when the real meaning is: "I love me, and I want to use you."

While we are sexual beings we are also social and spiritual beings. If our sexuality harms the social and spiritual parts of us, then we are not only sinning against God and against others but against ourselves. In Proverbs 6:31 the Bible asserts, "A man who commits adultery doesn't have any sense. He is just destroying himself" (GNB).

How do we enjoy God's gift of sexuality without destroying ourselves? Search the pages of the Bible, and you will find only one answer: Marriage. I'm not sure I can defend the notion that marriages are made in heaven. But I know that marriage is. This is God's way in which the most beautiful things we can know are produced. It is the way in which a potentially killing urge can be made into a blessing rather than a curse.

When time was just beginning, God looked at all he had made and said, "That's good. That's very good!" (Gen. 1:31). Yet something was missing. This peak of creation's pinnacle, this center of creation's circle was incomplete. So God created for Adam a "suitable" companion. They were to enjoy each other, enjoy God, and take charge and enjoy the world around them. This is God's pattern for marriage. He gave Eve one Adam and Adam one Eve. He declared that marriage is to involve male and female. It was Adam and Eve, not Adam and Fred.

Many students of history agree that this is a crucial matter to our national survival. Our hope lies in maintaining strong homes. If the home goes, our freedom goes. History has demonstrated with monotonous consistency that any people who lose respect for marital fidelity and give themselves up to an orgy of self-indulgence have no future. When "anything goes," everything is gone.

One last word must be added to the words *control* and *marriage*. That word is *grace*. In this society many homes are failing. You may be one who has experienced this tragic wreck on life's highway. Know for sure that to every such wreck God sends an ambulance, not a firing squad. Indeed divorce is a sin because it is a failure. That's what sin is—failure. Divorce may in some cases be unavoidable. It may be the lesser of two evils, but it is an evil. God's Word always calls us to look upon marriage vows with complete seriousness. Yet we never forget he is the Lord of grace, the God of the second chance. Ours is the glorious gospel of beginning again. He has never stopped loving you. When you come to him admitting failure and by faith claiming his cleansing, then acceptance, love, and peace are his gifts to you.

John 8:1-11 tells of a woman who had been caught in the act of adultery. She was crudely and cruelly brought to a meeting Jesus was addressing. When this woman was forcefully ushered into the presence of Christ, she probably had the same attitude you and I have when we are caught red-handed. She may have, at first, protested that there was nothing really wrong with what she had done. After all, why should society decide what two consenting adults should do? It is the normal pattern of human pride to react, when confronted with our sins, with more anger than sorrow.

I'm sure she was frightened. It's true the chances were remote that they'd really stone her to death, but they were talking about it. Then shame crept in, tardy as usual. Shame always seems to arrive late, but it stays longer.

What a strange mixture of question marks and exclamation points must have paraded through her mind as she heard Jesus turn the judgment from the accused to the accusers. By simply scratching a few words in the dirt he stripped them of their judicial robes of righteousness. Here we learn a good deal about the mind of our Lord. The grace of his love would not condemn her, nor would the salt of his righteousness condone her sin. Her sinful act could be forgiven, but it must also be forsaken. "Neither do I condemn thee: go, and sin no more" (v. 11).

First John 1:9 declares this truth to every guilt-ridden heart: "If we confess our sins, he is faithful and just to forgive us our sins, and to cleanse us from all unrighteousness."

8

Don't Steal Freedom From Yourself

Exodus 20:15

Life can be equated to a bicycle built for three. On the third seat, going along for the ride, is the person who does no peddling, no steering, and does not even notice the scenery. On the middle seat sits one who loves the ride, appreciates the scenery, thanks the one doing the peddling, but makes no personal contribution to the effort. On the front seat supplying all the power and direction sits the one representing the mighty minority of people who make things happen.

Margaret Slattery was one who made things happen. One day, in a slum area of Chicago, she met a boy named Freddy. Freddy was paralyzed from the waist down. His parents explained that an expensive operation offered the chance that Freddy might walk, but they simply couldn't afford the surgery. Margaret Slattery made Freddy's plight known to the nation. She diligently solicited the funds needed for the surgery. When the moment of truth came, when Freddy was to try his first steps, his parents said, "Miss Slattery, if Freddy can walk, we want him to take his first steps toward you. You made this possible." With great effort Freddy took two steps and fell into her arms. The miracle had happened! Freddy could walk!

Years later Margaret Slattery said, "I wish I could tell you Freddy is now standing on those legs doing surgery to help other children walk, but I can't say that. You see, Freddy is in federal prison because he committed a hideous crime against another." She went on to say, "Medical science can help a boy to walk, but only God can help him walk in the right direction."

The Ten Commandments are God's principles for walking in freedom's path, for walking in the right direction. The Sixth Commandment declares that if we are to keep free we will recognize that something is very special about another's life. Number seven asserts we are to recognize that something is sacred about another's wife or husband.

Now the Word declares that no society will last for long unless we see that something is sacred about another's property. Honesty and trust are the backbones of our economical system. Many banks are called trust companies, for that is what they exist upon. Our word *credit* comes from a word which means "to trust." If everyone decided not to pay what is owed, our system would collapse.

Probably the greatest cause of inflation is stealing. In Houston, Texas, it is estimated that one billion dollars per year is stolen in the stores. This is passed along to the paying customers in higher prices—one billion dollars in one city alone. Add to that the higher cost occasioned by workers who won't work, employees who steal from their companies, and you have a large chunk of higher prices. Hours could be consumed pointing out how the breaking of this commandment alone could cause this or any other nation to fall.

Benjamin Franklin declared, "Honesty is the best policy." God's Word is asserting what history is constantly underscoring: "Honesty is the only policy if we are to survive."

Our land is stalked by 1,001 varieties of thieves. It begins early as children hear parents brag about cheating on income tax or making a false claim to the insurance company.

Then the child starts to school and soon learns to cheat on

homework and tests. Twelve years later that child has stolen a diploma from the school and an education from himself.

When he goes to work, he steals from his employer by not working when on the job or by taking things home from the job. Once a maid told Charles Hadden Spurgeon she had been saved. "Is there any change in your life?" he asked. "Oh, yes," she declared, "I don't sweep dirt under the rug anymore."

Many in our country are stealing the affections of someone's wife or husband. This breaks specifically and pointedly the Seventh, Eighth, and Tenth Commandments; yet it is an accepted practice in our crumbling society. One girlie magazine once published this line: "Thou shalt not omit adultery."

It is stealing to take advantage of another's misfortune. When Jacob found Esau in a weakened condition because of his hunger, Jacob took advantage of the situation and stole his brother's birthright. A lot of stealing is done in the name of shrewdness.

Businesses which take advantage of human weaknesses steal from their society. The liquor industry is a case in point. In one year taxes paid by the liquor industry amounted to 18 billion dollars. In that same year it cost this nation 43 billion dollars to pay for problems occasioned by the presence of liquor in our society. The dollar loss is not so tragic as the knowledge that 205,000 deaths a year are traced to the problem of alcohol consumption. Now, let me quickly add that these figures are found in a carefully documented study made by our government; yet the bar owners are begging for longer hours in the name of "serving the public." You make half an effort to learn what this deadly and deceptive drug is doing to our nation, and you will conclude that anyone who sells or gives away beer, wine, and liquor is doing a great disservice to the public.

Did you ever steal another's reputation? Have you ever

spread slander about someone else? You might say, "I didn't start it, I just passed it on." Do you know what a "fence" in the underworld is? That's a person who receives stolen goods and sells them to someone else. Under law the "fence" is just as guilty as the person who stole the property. Do you ever "fence" stolen reputations? If so, you are just as guilty as the one who started the story.

Have you ever stolen from God? There are many ways we can do that. Malachi spells out one way in uncomfortable clarity:

Will a man rob God? Yet ye have robbed me. But ye say, wherein have we robbed thee? In tithes and offerings. Ye are cursed with a curse: for ye have robbed me, even this whole nation. Bring ye all the tithes into the storehouse, that there may be meat in my house, and prove me now herewith, saith the Lord of hosts, if I will not open you the windows of heaven, and pour you out a blessing, that there shall not be room enough to receive it (3:8-10).

It is not only possible to steal from God, but it is also possible to steal God's blessing from others. When Mark Twain married Olivia Langdon she was a most committed Christian, but Twain was clever and sharp with his words against her Christian practices. Later, there came into her life a very deep sorrow. He urged, "Livy, lean on your faith!" Sadly she said, "I can't, I don't have any left." To his dying day he was haunted by the fact that he had taken from her that which had meant so much.

Well, God's Word points up many ways to steal, but the central teaching here is that we are to respect the property rights of other people, all the while remembering that everything belongs to God.

This is one sin which often demands more than repentance, it also calls for restitution. If you have stolen goods or money from someone, you are to pay back more than you stole.

Remember the day in Jericho when, much to the consternation of the crowd, Jesus went home with Zacchaeus? Later on, we hear Zacchaeus say: "Lord, the half of my goods I give to the poor; and if I have taken any thing from any man . . . I restore him fourfold." Jesus replied, "This day is salvation come to this house" (Luke 19:8-9).

Our attitude toward the things God lets us use during this stay on earth is of supreme importance. One of our Lord's most famous stories is aimed at that very subject. He told of an unfortunate traveler who was mugged on the road between Jericho and Jerusalem. Thieves beat him, took his money, and left him lying in a ditch. In varying degrees each one of us is represented by the three groups of people in that story. There were the crooks saying, "I'll take from you. What's yours is mine. I'll take it." There were the calloused, the uncaring saying, "I'll keep from you. What's mine is mine. I'll keep it." And there was the one whom Christ said is to be our example, the caring, saying, "I'll give to you. What's mine is yours. I'll share it." God help us all to join the company of the caring.

We steal freedom from ourselves when we take, by any means, whatever belongs to another and whatever belongs to God. Benjamin Franklin was right, "Honesty is the best policy." In fact, it is the only policy if we are to survive.

9

Loose Talk Sinks Freedom

Exodus 20:16

In World War II a slogan in defense factories reminded people of the danger of carelessly sharing information the enemy could use. On most every wall you could see the words: "Loose Lips Sink Ships."

In Exodus 20:16 we are warned that loose talk sinks freedom. The command is, "Do not accuse anyone falsely" (GNB).

There can be no "government of the people, by the people, and for the people" unless the people are right. The Sixth, Seventh, Eighth, and Ninth Commandments are a part of the law of our nation. Indeed, our American system won't work unless enough people respect and keep these laws.

Sometimes I wish we'd never heard the word *morality*. The word carries with it an idea of moral opinion. You've heard it said, "Well, you have your set of morals, and I have mine." I wish we could look at the words *right* and *wrong*, not from a "moral" standpoint but a practical one. When conducting an experiment in a laboratory if it turns out as hoped, you say, "That's right." If it blows up in your face, you say, "That's wrong!"

You see, God is not saying, "Here are some ideas I want you to check out and see if they fit your life-style." He is saying, "Here are some principles which, if you will follow,

59

will make life work. If you don't follow them, life won't work."

If we are to be the first civilization in history to keep freedom, we must return to the Ninth Commandment, "Thou shalt not bear false witness against thy neighbour." Our legal system cannot work if witnesses do not "tell the truth, the whole truth, and nothing but the truth."

It is vital that we see how serious a matter our Lord considers the stewardship of speech to be. The Word declares:

These six things doth the Lord hate: yea, seven are an abomination unto him: A proud look, a lying tongue, and hands that shed innocent blood, an heart that deviseth wicked imaginations, feet that be swift in running to mischief, a false witness that speaketh lies, and he that soweth discord among brethren (Prov. 6:16-19).

Four of the seven things God hates refer to the wrongful use of the tongue. Jesus said in Matthew 12:36-37, "I say to you, that every careless word that men shall speak, they shall render account for it in the day of judgment. For by your words you shall be justified, and by your words you shall be condemned" (NASB).

Why? Didn't we say as youngsters, "Sticks and stones may break my bones, but words will never harm me"? It is not so, my friends. Words can kill. Lying has caused the greatest disasters in history. The serpent lied to Adam and Eve about the forbidden fruit, and all of mankind has suffered the agony of separation from God. Satan used lies to bring about the crucifixion of Christ. Drunken Nero set fire to Rome, then blamed the Christians, thus starting the cruel persecution of the early church. Hitler lied to the people of Germany. His false witness concerning the Jews alone caused six million deaths. The illustrations could be stated for hours, picturing the tragedy caused by lying.

Now we begin to understand. God hates lying because it hurts people. He hates anything that hurts others because he loves all people. God is love, and God is truth. Nothing but truth can come from love. If we tell untruths about others, it is life's surest sign that the God of love is not ruling our hearts.

We can hurt people terribly with our speech. Have you ever listened to yourself and others talk? I mean, really. You know, when I hear us talk I sometimes wonder if we'll have anything at all to say when we get to heaven. It is highly unlikely we'll be running down the administration. We won't be able to talk about how heaven has "gone to the dogs" and how it used to be in the "good ol' days." The weather will be perfect. We won't have any aches and pains. We won't be gossiping and sniping at others because surely the Lord is going to remove that poison from our systems. Well, you take away gunning at the administration, griping about the mess things are in, grumbling about the weather, groaning about our aches and pains, and gossiping about others and you've just about eliminated the totality of some folks' conversational ability.

It is possible to slander a person in other ways than blatant lies. There can be a subtle slander that is devastating, sort of "no-risk" lying. Satan is "the father of lies," says the Scripture (John 8:44), and he is the first one to teach this "safe" way to slander another. About Job, he said, "Does Job fear God for nothing?" (Job 1:9, NIV). The idea was planted that maybe Job's motive for serving God was less than perfect. You know how it goes, just asking questions which rip at others' reputations. "Have you noticed how well he's done financially since he was elected?" "Have you noticed how late he has been working since he got that new secretary?"

There are many ways we can hurt others with our speech, but have you ever thought about how much harm we can do to ourselves? By our speech we can bring the severe judgment of

God upon ourselves. Listen again to Matthew 12:36-37, "I say to you, that every careless word that men shall speak, they shall render account for it in the day of judgment. For by your words you shall be justified, and by your words you shall be condemned." Again, in the Sermon on the Mount, Jesus said, "Do not judge lest you be judged yourselves. For in the way you judge, you will be judged" (Matt. 7:1-2, NASB). I hope you read that loudly and clearly, my friend. God is saying, "If you are harsh, critical, and condemning toward others, then I will judge you in the same way." He declares this in many ways in the Bible. When our Lord talked about forgiving he said, "If you forgive men for their transgressions, your heavenly Father will also forgive you. But if you do not forgive men, then your Father will not forgive your transgressions" (Matt. 6:14-15, NASB).

When you are critical, judgmental, and untruthful in your attitude toward others, you do more than bring God's judgment on yourself. You destroy your own spirit. You become like a vulture who flies over beautiful mountains, trees, and streams but is only looking for some wounded or dead carcass to devour.

Well, what do we do? Is there a positive way to apply this principle to our lives?

For a starter, stop playing God. It's not your right or your ability to judge others. In a book titled *Mr. God, This is Anna,* a six-year-old reminds us that we see only the outside. Only God can see the inside of people.

Christians are to be motivated by love. If love rules your heart, you never want to hurt others. Before you say anything about anyone let your anticipated statements pass through these three gates: "Is it true? Do you really know?" Then, "Is it necessary? Why do you have to say it?" And last, "Is it kind?'' We are never ashamed of our speech if it passes those examinations.

Some of Paul's parting advice to the Philippian Christians is God's word to you and me: "Finally, brethren, whatever is true, whatever is honorable, whatever is right, whatever is pure, whatever is lovely, whatever is of good repute, if there is any excellence and if anything worthy of praise, let your mind dwell on these things" (4:8, NASB).

Above all, don't lie about your neighbor. Don't tell unnecessary truth if it will hurt him; then he probably won't lie about you or say things that hurt you. In this way you can live in peace and freedom.

10

Freedom Begins in Your Head

Exodus 20:17

Exodus 20:17 states: "You shall not covet your neighbor's house; you shall not covet your neighbor's wife or his male servant or his female servant or his ox or his donkey or anything that belongs to your neighbor."

My late friend Grady Nutt used to be a regular on *Hee Haw*. He told of going to a small Christian college several years ago. He said it was located five miles from any known sin. "The school had three rules," said Grady. "You won't smoke, you won't drink, and you won't want to." He said, "I was dismissed for wanting to."

Well, wanting to is where it all begins. This commandment recognizes the titanic truth that all good and bad begins in your head. Your life will be a success or a failure in direct proportion to that which you desire.

I heard a teacher once when I was in high school say you become what you think about all day long. There is real truth in that. Of course you don't want to make it crawl on all fours. If I became what I thought about as a teenager I probably would have become a girl. But in Proverbs there is a verse that says, "As [a man] thinketh in his heart, so is he" (23:7).

It's literally true, what you set the affections of your heart and mind upon, what you desire, will have a great deal to do with what you become.

What does *covet* mean? It means to desire earnestly. Now it is an amoral word. *Coveting* can be either bad or good. Paul told the Corinthian Christians to covet the best gifts. In the Sermon on the Mount, Jesus said, "Blessed are they which do hunger and thirst after righteousness" (Matt. 5:6).

Faith has never been a synonym for laziness. Remember the commercials of a few years back in which one milk company advertised that their milk "comes from contented cows"? A contemporary company then retorted, "Our cows are never contented. They keep trying to do better."

When our Lord tells us to be contented with what we have, he is simply warning us not to let life's furniture make a fool of us. He is not telling us not to do better.

It is not coveting or desiring earnestly that is forbidden here. What is expressly forbidden is desiring earnestly your neighbor's property or his wife or her husband. It isn't necessarily wrong to desire a home or a spouse. It's to want to take someone or something away from someone else that is wrong. It may not be wrong to want a beautiful car, but it is definitely wrong to want your neighbor's car. It is perfectly natural to desire a wife, but it is supremely sinful to desire your neighbor's wife.

As Jesus applied this principle to Christian living he went deeper. He combined our desires for things with the First Commandment, "Thou shalt have no other gods before me" (Ex. 20:3). In so doing he warned that desiring things more than desiring right standing with God is one of life's largest blunders.

We talk of standards of living and mean nothing about standards or living. We often talk about how much a man is worth when we speak only of how much he has. We must be constantly warned that it is a sin to make the acquiring of money and its derivatives our consuming passion.

In younger days I bought a book entitled *Think and Grow*

Rich. Now, it is not a bad book. It contains some very good advice, even for those who do not think exclusively in dollar signs. The foreword said a great secret was written between the lines, and as a reader when I discovered the secret I was well on my way to being rich.

The secret was easily found. It was greed—grubby, grasping, greed. The book, *Think and Grow Rich,* said all you were supposed to think about is growing rich. With that in mind, then, we need to pay heed to what Jesus said about Christian principles of possessing. These are found in Matthew 6.

Lay not up for yourselves treasures upon earth, where moth and rust doth corrupt, and where thieves break through and steal: But lay up for yourselves treasures in heaven, where neither moth nor rust doth corrupt, or where thieves do not break through nor steal: For where your treasure is, there will your heart be also (vv. 19-21).

Here our Lord presents three principles of possessing. The first is this: temporary holdings do not constitute real riches. That which can be lost is not really owned. No man is rich to whom the grave brings bankruptcy.

I heard a man from Latvia tell what happened when the Communists took over his country. He was a member of a vastly wealthy family whose chief holding was a giant, capital city department store. "The day the Communists came," he said, "we were able to take out of the store only the clothes we were wearing. We left everything we owned in Latvia and fled for our freedom."

Here our Lord says, "Because I love you I do not want you to spend your short but valuable lives piling up temporary treasure. Haven't you lived long enough to learn that just about the time a man says, 'I've got it made,' time runs out on him? Don't you know that life's treasures are always being eaten by the moths of depreciation, wasted by the rust of inflation, and stolen by the thousand and one varieties of thieves that inhabit this earth? Temporary holdings do not constitute real riches."

Here is the second principle: eternal investment is wisest, "Lay up for yourselves treasures in heaven" (v. 20). God wants us to possess. He wants us to have, but he wants us to have the best. Hear him say, "If you keep your fortune on earth, you have made a fortune and stored it in a place where you cannot hold it. Make your fortune, but store it in a place where you can keep it. Invest it in the kingdom of God and let it draw interest compounded throughout eternity."

Is money that important? Why all this musing about so mundane a matter as money? Well, here is the third principle: we always look after our investments. "Where your treasure is, there will your heart be also" (v. 21).

Your treasure itself is not of the greatest importance, but what it does to your heart is important. This is why the love of money is called the root of all kinds of evil (1 Tim. 6:10). It can pull you down to a low level and change your life to a frustration of temporariness where your every desire, every move, and every joy is directly related to the condition of your bank account or the stock market. But if invested in heaven it can anchor your soul. It can fix your attention on the eternal and keep your heart in the condition God wants for it and give you peace and happiness.

It is always good to remind ourselves that our Lord says what he says out of a motive of making our lives better. Coveting things to the point that it becomes a great passion even above God is wrong because it hurts us, not just because it offends God.

What does it mean to you? It makes you unhappy and tense. In the Old Testament King Ahab owned every bit of land in sight except one small vineyard which was possessed by a man named Naboth (1 Kings 21:1-4). Naboth had inherited the land from his parents. It was sacred to him, and he was not going to let it go; Ahab became a pouting, crying little child, lying with his back to everyone else because there was some little piece of land that he did not have. Because of his covetousness he committed a great sin.

There was Haman in the Book of Esther, a man whom everyone in town bowed to and respected. But Haman only had eyes for Mordecai who had not bowed to him, and this clouded his whole life. Haman's covetous desire to be the ruler of everyone around caused him great distress and great harm (3:1-6).

There was King David who had beautiful wives and yet lusted after someone else's wife. He committed the sin of adultery and caused great problems to come upon his life (2 Sam. 11:1-5).

Covetousness will lead you down an unhappy trail. It leads to a decaying of character. If the supreme desire of your life is just to get things, especially things that others have, then it will lead you to become a liar; it will lead you to adultery; it will lead you to theft. It destroys the opportunity for life's best. I guess the greatest problem of all is that if you want only things, you sink to the level of things, and you miss so much of what it means to be made in the image of God.

On a tombstone in the northern part of the United States there is a telling epitaph. It says: "Born a human being. Died a wholesale grocer."

How do we overcome covetousness? Our Lord reminds us that it is never enough just to drive the thought out. You must put a positive one in.

How did you forget the boy or girl you were madly in love with in high school? Why, you met someone else. How do you get rid of the greed that destroys your life or the inordinate desire for things that drives you to be less than you ought to be? Why, you meet Someone who changes that life. His name is the Lord Jesus Christ.

You know, the apostle Paul was an extremely ambitious man. Yet he's the one who later made the statement, "I have learned to be content in whatever circumstances I am" (Phil. 4:11, NASB).

Now he wasn't content with his world. We know that because he kept trying to change it. He was not content with himself. He wrote in Philippians 3:13, "I count not myself to have apprehended," meaning "I haven't arrived." He said, "This one thing I do, forgetting those things which are behind, and reaching forth unto those things which are before, I press toward the mark for the prize of the high calling of God in Christ Jesus" (vv. 13-14). But Paul said that he was contented with his Master. He was contented with the One whom he had made supreme Lord of his life and who strengthened him (Phil. 4:11-13).

The greatest problem with the things of this world is that they crowd God off the throne of your life. Jesus said in the Sermon on the Mount, "No man can serve two masters, you cannot serve God and mammon."

How do you overcome the corruption of covetousness in your life? You simply do what this chorus commands:

> Turn your eyes upon Jesus,
> Look full in his wonderful face,
> And the things of earth will grow strangely dim
> In the light of his glory and grace.[1]

---

1. From "Turn Your Eyes upon Jesus" written by Helen H. Lemmel, 1922. Copyright 1922. Renewal 1950 by H. H. Lemmel. Assigned to Singspiration, Inc.

11

The Freedom to Go for It

Matthew 25:14-30

Our Lord did not tell this story to spotlight the five-talent man or the two-talent man. The revealing of their reward stands out in a wonderful way to say that any who use rightly the life and time and goods that God has given will receive a "Well done, thou good and faithful servant" (v. 21).

He focuses our attention on this one-talent servant and boldly underscores a truth that is titanic in God's Word—to refuse to serve is a great sin. This one-talent man shows us how to be wicked without really trying. With elaborate skill Christ paints the portrait of a good man who was wicked because he was good for nothing.

How harshly the man is reprimanded in verse 26, "Thou wicked and slothful servant." Only sixteen times is this original word used in the New Testament. Six times it refers directly to the devil himself. Seven times it is used in a general sense, speaking of a wicked generation or a wicked imagination. Only two other times is this word used of a particular person outside that of Satan. This word that Jesus used for "wicked" could be translated "malignant." It is indeed a strong word. What did this man do to be called "bad, malignant, wicked" and to be placed in the same category as Satan himself?

He was not a wasteful man. He didn't squander foolishly the master's money. We are not told of any immorality, drinking habits, lawbreaking or related things, so this is not why he is called wicked. He was not a prodigal; never once did he even dream of taking the Lord's talent and running off to a far country.

As we ponder this parable we are made to see that this is the saga of a useless man. A drama of doing nothing. It warns us that we can be wicked without really trying. We are wicked when we do not use what God has given us. We are wicked when we lack the courage of adventure. Whenever we are guilty of the wickedness of uselessness, we lose what we have.

We are wicked when we do not use what God has given us. It is easy to see that you and I probably would not have called this man wicked, but it is undeniably plain to see that Jesus did. He was wicked not because of what he did but because of what he did not do.

How consistent is this to the truths Christ has presented all along. You remember how Jesus rebuked the barren fig tree, not because it bore bad fruit or sorry fruit but because it bore no fruit at all.

Remember how seriously Jesus told of the man who was beaten, robbed, and left dying in a ditch on that rough road between Jerusalem and Jericho? He told that story to remind us that the real thieves were the priest and the Levite who walked by on the other side of the road and did nothing. They were the real thieves. They robbed that man of their mercy. They were the most wicked people in that story.

Be it indelibly etched on the wall of our awareness that God has us in mind when we read, "To him that knoweth to do good, and doeth it not, to him it is sin" (Jas. 4:17).

Often we talk of immoral people. Is there anything more immoral than to know the great secret of victory over sin and over death and not tell it? What would we think of a doctor who knew how to cure cancer and kept quiet about it? How wicked, how wrong, how cruel. Jesus says this world is dying and you and I as Christians have the remedy, and for us to do nothing with this cure that has been placed in our hands is wickedness.

The strangest of all creatures on God's earth is the Christian bandit. He plunders and loots the days of his life and does not seek to use what God has given him to serve God. To take the life God gives us and use it as we please can be nothing short of embezzlement. To every Christian the Word proclaims, "Ye are not your own, ye are bought with a price."

We are taking the first step toward wickedness when, like this man, we do not see that our talent is needed. I can hear him say, "Well, that five-talent fellow and that two-talent man ought to do something for God, but my one little talent just is not needed." Our Lord's reaction to such an attitude is stern anger. Everyone is important to Kingdom work. We will never do for our Lord all that he intends until everyone does his part.

We are walking in the wickedness of doing nothing when we fail to see that every talent is precious. The one-talent man depreciated his gift. He didn't think it was important.

One of the many surprises of the messages of Jesus is his insistence on the worth of what we might call "small service." He talked of the high value of a cup of cold water given in his name. Of the law he said, "Till heaven and earth pass, one jot or one tittle shall in no wise pass from the law, till all be fulfilled" (Matt. 5:18). He said that to perform deeds like feeding the hungry and visiting the prisoners is one of the best indications of our love for him. He warned it is not within human wisdom to judge when a deed is great or small. One day he watched the people making their offerings at the Temple and stated that the woman who gave the least amount of money had made the largest gift. It is not within our knowing to tell if a deed is large or small. It is within our great responsibility to do what we can for our Lord. We are wicked when we do not.

We are wicked when we lack the courage of adventure. Hear the man of our story as he explained in the day of reckoning, "I was afraid. I was so timid I did absolutely nothing."

There is a large danger that this may happen in the church today. Christ has challenged us to go into our city, our world, and reach people—teach people—win people. "This is your work," he said. "Use all the courage and daring and imagination at your disposal to extend your outreach, so that at my coming I can say to you, 'Well done, good and faithful servant.'"

What an exciting thing to think of how the church began. Look at that early church. Paul reflected upon the membership of the church at Corinth and said, "Not many wise men after the flesh, not many mighty, not many noble, are called" (1 Cor. 1:26). But God used these people without worldly wisdom, without the might of money or organized strength, and without the prestige of noble position to change the world. Why? Because they were people of a daring faith. They were adventurous Christians. They never thought of saying, "I know we ought to, but I don't think we can do that," or "I don't know, we never did it that way before." They just dedicated their imagination and their daring and their faith and God did the impossible through them!

While many Christians of today are bogged down with a sense of the impossible, there are yet to be found God's people who have a keen sense of the possible. People who say with Paul, "I can do everything through him who gives me strength" (Phil. 4:13, NIV). People who know they can do anything God wants them to, do!

Now in relation to our own work for Christ there is the danger that we may commit the sin of the unprofitable servant. We can be wicked by simply not exhibiting the faith of daring adventure. God has honored us by putting us in a position to reach our friends for Christ. But if we take this opportunity and bury it in the sorry sod of unconcern or selfishness, we are indeed wicked people.

Thank God that there are yet to be found folk with faith and people with a desire to go all out for him. Know this, dear follower of Jesus, any time you want things to stay just like they are you are committing the sin of the man who was called wicked because he shrank from risk, even though he knew that nothing is ever gained without it.

Now here is the third thing. Whenever we are guilty of the wickedness of uselessness, we lose what we have. "Take the talent from him," said the Lord, "and give it to the one who has the ten talents" (Matt. 25:28, NIV).

Be this an indictment to every soul. God gives you your talent to use. If you do not use it, you will lose it. God gives to people and churches and nations opportunities to use. If we do not do so, he takes the opportunity away and gives it to people who do care.

The world is littered with lost talent. You once had the ability to sing, but you didn't use it, and you lost it. You once had the ability to care, and your heart could be burdened with concern; but you didn't act on that concern, and now you are hard as nails.

The will of one infidel farmer shocked all at the hearing when it reflected his wishes that all his farm be given to the devil—lock, stock, and barrel. After much study, those who executed the will decided that the best way to carry out the infidel farmer's wishes was simply to leave it alone. Let no one paint the buildings, no one hoe the weeds, and no one till the soil. Soon the rotting barns and house, rusting machinery, high weeds, and eroded fields proved that indeed the farm had gone to the devil—by default!

Many a life goes to the devil in the same way. If you want to destroy your home, you don't have to beat your wife, just don't tell her you love her. Never thank her for the clean clothes in your closet or for the good food she prepares. Just don't care. If you want to destroy your children, you don't have to pour booze down their throats or shoot drugs into their veins. Just don't care who their friends are or when they come in at night. If you want to destroy your church, you don't have to burn it down or blow it up, just don't care. When the class you teach or the teacher in your class is counting on you— when the Lord is counting on you—just don't care, and you will destroy your church.

How will it be to face the Lord in that day when we have been guilty of the wickedness of uselessness? Hear this unprofitable man say, "I knew thee that thou art an hard man, reaping where thou has not sown, and gathering where thou has not strawed" (v. 24). With that sort of knowledge we'd expect him to say, "I knew you were a hard man, so I dug in. Those other fellows were lazy. They just doubled what you gave them, but I tripled mine. I knew, so I really went to work." But he didn't say that. He said, "I knew, but I did nothing."

How is it going to sound someday when we stand in the presence of Jesus, see the scars on his hands and feet and side, the print of the thorns on his brow, and tell him why we didn't serve him; why we did not give ourselves in faithful service? How do you think our excuses will sound in that day? "Lord, I knew that you died on the cross for me. I knew that you would supply all the strength for me to serve you in an unlimited way, but. . . . " What in eternity can we say that will make any sense?

12

Born Free!

Where did the words *born again* originate? What do they mean? While the phrase wonderfully describes the Christian experience of salvation, it is found in the Bible only in John 3:1-8. It was our Lord Christ who said, "You must be born again" (v. 8, NASB). He spoke the words in a conversation with a man named Nicodemus.

This puzzled man came to Christ one night, hoping to find some light. Bible commentators galore have crawled on "all fours," looking for a reason why Nicodemus came at night. Some say he did not want to be seen with Christ, so he sought the cover of darkness. Others assert he came at night because Jesus was so busy with the needs of the multitudes in the daytime. Maybe Nicodemus himself was too busy in the daylight hours.

It could just as well be that Nicodemus came that night because he did not want to wait until the next morning. Perhaps he had confronted Christ earlier in the day or had a conversation with a follower of Christ. And he detected in that presence something for which he had always looked but had never found—an undefined quality of life he longed to have. He tried to sleep but could not. Being the wise man that he was, he determined to do something. He refused to count sheep. He would, instead, talk to the shepherd. So he sought Christ out in the dark of the night.

What did Nicodemus want? We might better ask, What did

Nicodemus have? And the answer: Nicodemus had everything. He was not a man of great sin. He was not a man of low character nor of immoral habit nor of poor education. He was the best man institutional religion could make. He was cultured, loyal, high-minded, generous, and devoutly religious. He had social power and respect. He had influence and position. This "master of Israel" had the authority and prestige of the supreme court of his land behind him. He had wealth and security. In addition, he was clean, reserved, superior, removed, dignified, and rich. He had *all* his religion could give him—all the best religion of his time could give him—and he was hungry. Like all his kind, he was hungry. See his hunger! It runs out and down between his sentences, pregnant with meaning: "We know thou art a teacher come from God" (3:2). "How can a man be born when he is old?" (v. 4). "How can these things be?" (v. 9).

In these lines of Holy Scripture, our Lord reveals the secret of life to every confused soul who has tried his best. He speaks to all the tired people who have aching sides and panting breath from trying to run well in life but have never sensed the experience of winning the race. The conversation has three phases: face-to-face, mind to mind, and heart to heart.

This interview begins as Jesus and Nicodemus stand face-to-face. It could be subtitled "Teacher, Teach Me." Verse 1 gives us the credentials of this important person—a Pharisee, a ruler of the Jews. Verse 2 indicates his great respect for and high impression of our Lord Christ. "Rabbi, we know you must be a teacher come from God. There is simply no other way to explain how you do what you do." Nicodemus had come to this impressive Teacher looking for the latest word from God. He came on a purely intellectual basis, looking for some new teaching, some exciting saying, some motto by which life's secrets could be revealed.

But the answer of Christ to all who seek God's truth on that level crashes across all human thinking. Across all its religions, philosophies, theologies, the revealed Word of God asserts, "Ye must be born again."

This is a personal word. Nicodemus opened the conversation by making a mistake all too common. He tried to lose himself in the crowd. "We know that you are a teacher come from God."

Christ quickly brought this conversation back to a one-to-one basis. "You must . . . ," he said. He can do nothing for us until we come singularly into the open. Of all the prayers he heard prayed, the one Christ most complimented was the sincere cry, "Lord, be merciful to me a sinner." He can do business on that level.

Nicodemus also made a mistake that crops up today as a hardy perennial. "You are a teacher come from God," he said. Not so! He is not a teacher come from God. He is God come down to teach. The most common misconception I find is a supposed enlightened sweetness which sees Christ as one of the world's great teachers. For anyone who knows how to read and think, this is a totally impossible position. He is either the only Son of God, the only Savior, the only way to fellowship with God, or he is a fraud. For he claimed these things about himself. He is unique—unlike any other person who ever lived.

He is certainly not just a teacher come from God. He is God come down to teach. And his word to Nicodemus, to you, to me is: "You don't need something new to think or something new to say or something new to feel or something new to do. You need to be a new creature. 'You must be born again.'"

The next phase of coming to new life is mind to mind. "Lord, lead me."

Nicodemus was not arguing but, rather, wondering how it could be. He was saying: "You talk about this fundamental change which is so necessary. I know it is necessary, but in my experience it is so impossible. There is nothing I'd like more, but you might as well tell me—a full-grown man—to enter into my mother's womb and be born all over again." It was not the desirability but the possibility that plagued him.

He was not contradicting Jesus, he was just saying: "How can I go back to prenatal days and start over again? Here I am, the result of what I did an hour ago and all through these years."

If that is the way you feel, then hear our Lord's reply: "Don't let your intellect throw you at this point. You don't understand the wind either, but there it is."

You don't understand physical birth, but it happens. Don't marvel at this being born again as though it is impossible. If God can give life, he can add life. There is nothing more impossible in being born again than in being born at all. You can't really understand your first birth, but the Author of life gave it to you. Can't you trust him to give you your second birth, too? What did Christ come to this world for? To give life. "I am come," he kept saying, "that you might have life, and have it more abundantly." It is not more knowledge you need, it is more life.

Our Lord was simply stating that we don't need to add something to our lives. We need to start over again.

"But, Preacher," someone may say, "you can't change human nature." That's true, you can't, but God can. Second Corinthians 5:17 boldly claims: "If any man be in Christ, he is a new creature: old things are passed away; behold, all things are become new."

A caterpillar can change to a butterfly. Most do not. They

die before they change. But for flying, it is not an improved caterpillar that is needed; it is a butterfly. Not a caterpillar of finer color or more rapid movement of large proportions, it is a new creature that is needed.

One day a caterpillar climbs up into a tree where nature throws a fiber robe around him. He goes to sleep, and in a few weeks he emerges a beautiful butterfly. So a person distressed, discouraged, unhappy, hounded by conscience, driven by passion, ruled by selfishness can come to Christ by faith and emerge a new man.

Nicodemus was marveling at the miracles of Christ. And our Lord said to him, "Nicodemus, you can become one of my best miracles. You can be born again. You can have new life from above!" So can you, my friend. Remember the song, "It Took a Miracle." He can perform that miracle in any willing life.

Face-to-face, mind to mind, heart to heart, Savior, save me. That's the next step. There comes a crucial moment in the hour of a soul's awakening in which he stops discussing Christianity and experiences it. Christ is not only someone to know about, he is someone to know.

It is certainly important to have an intellectual grasp of the orb of Christian truth, but it is most important to have a vital experience with the living Christ.

When a person undergoes treatment from a doctor; when he has to have an operation; when he is given medicine to take, he does not need to know the anatomy of the human body, the scientific effect of the anesthetic, or the way in which the drug works on his body in order to be cured. Ninety-nine out of every one hundred accept the cure without being able to say how it was brought about. There is a sense in which Christianity is like that. The Great Physician has diagnosed the cure: "For God so loved the world, that he gave his only begotten

Son, that whoever believeth in him should not perish, but have everlasting life" (John 3:16).

The wisdom required is that which says: "I place my sin-sick soul in the hands of the Great Physician, trusting him to bring about the cure."

13

Freedom Forever

Matthew 25:31 ff.

We hear a lot of talk about life's highway. Maybe that's what it is, a one-way road where sometimes the scenery is drab and dull, and we almost go to sleep at the wheel; then all of a sudden the next curve brings some surprise scenery—some great, good thing we never suspected. On life's road there are bumps jarring us to our breaking point; there are detours of doubt, and often we find ourselves following in the same ruts that led others to get stuck in the mud of senseless living.

Maybe it is all right to talk of life as a highway. Jesus stated one day that he was the only way, the only real road to the riches of eternity.

If life is a road, then Christ is continually saying, "I want to tell you what is on down the road—farther than you can see right now. I want to prepare you for what is coming, for what you simply cannot avoid."

Christ tells us here of the fact of facing God. All roads do not lead to heaven, but all roads do lead to judgment. The parable of the sheep and goat judgment is the last in a series Christ was telling to encourage the saved and warn the lost of the road ahead.

In Matthew 24 he spoke of the fact that the coming of the Son of man would be when the world was not expecting it and that it would mean judgment upon men. He used as an illustration the experience of the people of the day of Noah. People in that day were eating, drinking, marrying, and giving in marriage until the day Noah entered the ark. They ignored impending judgment until the flood came and took them away. The emphasis appears to be that they were so involved in the ordinary things of everyday life they were not expecting anything unusual. Even though Noah preached to them of God's judgment, even though every blow of his hammer was a warning that judgment was coming, they were so involved in ordinary affairs that they paid no attention to the coming judgment of God. With dramatic suddenness it came and took them out of the world. Jesus said it would be that way when he comes again. He will come suddenly upon those engaged in ordinary affairs of life, and his coming will mean judgment.

In James 5:8-9, we are warned that the judge is already standing at the door. Paul comforted the Christians and warned the lost with the words, "The Lord is at hand" (Phil. 4:5).

In Matthew 22 Jesus tells of a wedding feast. All were bidden to come, but one came improperly dressed. The command was given to bind him, hand and foot, and cast him into outer darkness, "There shall be weeping and gnashing of teeth" (v. 13). When God comes in that day and one does not wear the garment of righteousness presented through the shed blood of Jesus Christ, that one shall be cast into the outer darkness of separation from God. In the story of the ten virgins in Matthew 25, Jesus again paints a vivid picture of some who were not ready for the master to come. They beat on the door and said, "Lord, Lord, open to us." And the stern, final reply rang back, "Verily I say unto you, I know you not" (vv. 11-12).

The final story in this series of illustrations is this well-known story of the sheep and goat judgment. This is the climax to all Jesus said about his coming again. When the Son of man comes, he will divide people as a shepherd divides the animals that are before him, putting the sheep on one side and the goats on the other. On one side the Son of man who is spoken of as a King will put those who are his followers, those who have trusted him for their salvation and whose lives have proven this committal. On the other side are the people who have not trusted Christ as Lord and Savior, and upon them he will place a sentence of judgment, and they will go away into eternal punishment. The ones who are sheep will go away into eternal life. It is a story which warns that when he comes again we must be prepared; there will be no other chance given.

It certainly is not true that all roads lead to heaven, but it is true that all roads lead to judgment. Your life's road and mine will inevitably lead us to that place of accounting. We must prepare for the day we will face God.

Then the King will say to those on His right, "Come, you who are blessed of My Father, inherit the kingdom prepared for you from the foundation of the world.
"For I was hungry, and you gave Me something to eat; I was thirsty, and you gave Me drink; I was a stranger, and you invited Me in; naked, and you clothed Me; I was sick, and you visited Me; I was in prison, and you came to Me."
Then the righteous will answer Him, saying, "Lord, when did we see You hungry, and feed You, or thirsty, and give You drink? And when did we see You a stranger, and invite You in, or naked, and clothe You? And when did we see You sick, or in prison, and come to You?"
And the King will answer and say to them, "Truly I say to you, to the extent that you did it to one of these brothers of Mine, even the least of them, you did it to Me" (Matt. 25:34-40, NASB).

Now Christ is not saying that taking care of the needs of people who are hungry, thirsty, naked, sick, and imprisoned is the way of salvation; but it is the way of a Christian. If doing things like this could save us, then the cross would be totally unnecessary. There are too many passages declaring that the saving grace of God cannot be earned by works, bought by money, taken by might, or learned by mind to mislead us at this point. What Christ is saying here is emphasized by a statement of his at another time, "You will know them by their fruits" (Matt. 7:20, NASB).

Our Lord is underscoring the fact that Christ makes a difference in a person's life. When one truly repents of sin and comes with trusting faith to the foot of that cross begging for salvation, then Christ saves him and something happens in that person. It is totally impossible to link your life to Christ and ever be the same again!

It is possible to shake hands with a Baptist preacher and still be the same. It is possible to experience a feeling of nostalgia occasioned by the hearing of a church bell or to incur a pensive mood while standing in a country churchyard or experience a nebulous sense of wonder cast by the eerie glow of candelabra and still go away the same. One may have a religion which only allows God a place in the scheme of things and still be the same person. You may know just about all there is to know about doctrines and post a score of ninety-five on a test on the tenets of the Christian faith. You may be able to shed a tear at a funeral or cast a silent ballot in heaven's favor or sometimes get on the religious bandwagon and give three rousing cheers for the church and still be the same person, but no one can give self unreservedly to Jesus Christ and ever be the same again. Christ makes a difference in life. Paul stated it, "Therefore if any man be in Christ, he is a new creature" (2 Cor. 5:17).

Our Lord is saying that this delightful difference will show in our service to others. Henry Van Dyke wrote about *The Other Wise Man*.

His name was Artaban. He set out to follow the star and took with him a sapphire, a ruby, and a pearl beyond price as gifts for the King. He was riding hard to meet his three friends,

Caspar, Melchior, and Balthazar at the agreed meeting place. The time was short; they would leave if he were late. Suddenly he saw a dim figure on the ground before him. It was a traveler stricken with fever. If he stayed to help he would be too late. He did stay—he helped the man. But now he was alone. He needed camels and bearers to help him across the desert because he had missed his friends and their caravan. He had to sell his sapphire to get them because he had helped the man, and he was sad that the king would never have his gem.

So he journeyed, and in due time he came to Palestine and then to Bethlehem, but again he was too late. Joseph and Mary and Baby Jesus had gone. Then there came the soldiers to carry out Herod's command that the children should be slain. Artaban was lodging in a home where there was a little child he had come to love. The tramp of the soldiers was heard at the door; the weeping of stricken mothers could be heard. Artaban stood in the doorway, tall and dark. He had the ruby in his hand. When the captain came, Artaban bribed him with his ruby not to enter. The child was saved. The mother was overjoyed; but the ruby was gone, and Artaban was sad, for as he thought that the King would never have his ruby now. For years he wandered, looking for the King.

More than thirty years afterward he came to Jerusalem. There was a crucifixion that day. And when Artaban heard of this Jesus who was being crucified, he sounded like the wondrous King. He started out to Calvary. Maybe his pearl, the loveliest pearl in all the world, could buy the life of the King. Down the street fled a girl from a band of soldiers. "My father is in debt, and they are taking me to sell me as a slave to pay the debt. Save me." Artaban hesitated, then sadly he took out his pearl, gave it to the soldiers, bought the girl's freedom, and she was safe. All of a sudden the skies were dark; there was an earthquake and a flying tile hit Artaban on the head. He sank half-conscious on the ground. The girl pillowed his head on her lap. Suddenly his lips began to move, "Not so, my Lord: For when saw I thee an hungered?" [v. 37] "Three-and-thirty years have I looked for thee; but I have never seen thy face, nor ministered to thee, my King." And then like a whisper from very far away there came a low, sweet voice, *"Verily I say unto thee, Inasmuch as thou hast done it unto one of the least of these my brethren, thou hast done it unto me."* And Artaban smiled in death because he knew the King had received his gifts.

Our Lord would say, "When you walk life's road with me you will be very concerned about serving those whom I love."

The Bible has warned us that all of us must face the judgment of God. We know of the fact of facing God, and this will reveal the reality of our faith. Now the future is clearly foretold. Up until this point every person is traveling the same road; every road leads to this facing of God, but there are two roads. In verse 46 Christ spoke of these two roads, "and these [the lost] shall go away into everlasting punishment: but the righteous into life eternal."

So then the future is clearly foretold for every person. Those who have linked their lives by faith and committal to Christ are promised the joys of eternal life. The child of God is going home. Those who have refused to live for God but rather live for themselves, those who have neglected or put off the decision to accept eternal life in Jesus Christ, are going to destruction. Unless your life has been surrendered to Christ and you have been saved by taking him as Savior, then you are on a short highway to oblivion.

A recent newspaper item told of the tragic death of a young man. Driving at high speed one night, he crashed through a road barrier to be crushed at the bottom of a deep gorge. The bridge across the gorge had been torn away to be replaced by a new one. The tragedy was compounded by the fact that the young man worked with the crew which was constructing the new bridge. He should have known better, but he did not. Apparently he thought he was on another road. What appeared to be a highway of happiness was instead one of death.

It is so with everyone who has not been forgiven of sin through Christ. You know better. You have been told over and over again that Jesus is the only way, but you have continued on the highway into oblivion. One day you will reach the end and plunge into the bottomless gorge of everlasting punishment. In Proverbs 14:12 we find this wisdom, "There is a way which seemeth right unto a man, but the end thereof are the ways of death." Quit trying to do it your way. Do it God's way, and he can bring peace and happiness to your heart.

14

How Your Freedom Was Won

1 Corinthians 15

One of the most exciting chapters in the Bible is 1 Corinthians 15. It tells us that Jesus Christ, our Lord, has done something great. God has done many great things.

Think about the rotation of the earth. This globe is now moving on its axis at the rate of 1,000 MPH. If it turned 100 miles an hour, days and nights here would be 1000 percent as long. The sun would burn up the vegetation every day. If any survived, it would freeze in the long night. And there is the sun. It has a surface temperature of 12,000 degrees, and the earth is far enough away to be benefitted by its terrific heat. If the sun emitted only one half of its radiation, we would freeze. If it gave off one half more, we would roast alive. Focus on the slant of the earth—twenty-three degrees. If there were any difference the vapors from the seas would freeze all of the continents. If the moon were only 50,000 miles away, rather than its present distance, our tides would be so titanic that twice each day the continents would be submerged. Think about the crust of the earth—a few feet thicker, and there would be no life because there would be no oxygen. And the thinness of the atmosphere—only a little thinner, and all the millions of meteors now burning themselves out in space would pound this earth into oblivion.

God has been at work in history. He opened the Red Sea for his people; he caused the walls of Jericho to fall; he stopped the

mouths of lions for Daniel; he halted the course of the seasons
for the prophet; he fed Elijah in his need; he defeated Napoleon
with a snowflake and saved England with a fog at Dunkirk.
God has been busy in history.

To think of what God has done in Christ floods our hearts
with gratitude—our Lord loving us, dying for us. But the
greatest thing of all is what Jesus Christ does in us when we
receive him as Lord and Master of our lives. Knowing Jesus
Christ makes all the difference in two worlds.

The apostle Paul begins 1 Corinthians 15 with the avowal that
our gospel is based on facts. They are: Jesus Christ died for our
sins; they buried him; and he rose again. These facts become a
gospel for us, says the Bible, because Jesus Christ died for our
sins, just as the Scripture said he would. They buried him
because he was dead. And on the third day he came out of his
grave, just as he predicted he would.

The practical and pragmatic apostle goes on to say that of
the 500 people who saw the risen Christ, most were still alive
at the writing of this Corinthian letter and could verify those
facts. And for fifty-four verses Paul expounds what it means to
know a living Lord.

Then Paul caps it all off by even shaking his fist in the face
of death and chiding, "O death, where is thy sting? O grave,
where is thy victory? The sting of death is sin; and the strength
of sin is the law. But thanks be to God, which giveth us the
victory through our Lord Jesus Christ" (vv. 55-57). Is there
one word that ought to characterize the Christian's life? There
is. That word is *victory*.

I want us to hang our thoughts on these three hooks. To
know our Lord is to have victory over sin, victory in life, and
victory over time.

Jesus Christ gives us victory over sin. Can you imagine how
thousands of years ago the Great Physician, our Lord himself,

laid out the diseased body of mankind on the operating table of the world. With his scalpel—his word—sharper than any two-edged sword, he cut deeply into humanity's soul and there laid bare a malignant growth. "O Great Physician," we ask nervously, "what's wrong with us?" His diagnosis, penned in Romans 3:23, asserts, "All have sinned, and come short of the glory of God."

"Well, Lord, is sin serious? Is it a bad disease?"

Once again, the sad diagnosis is given, "The wages of sin is death." But before he takes a breath, the Great Healer of souls announces, "But the gift of God is eternal life through Jesus Christ our Lord" (Rom. 6:23).

Do you catch the thrust of that? He didn't come just to diagnose the disease. He came to provide the cure.

Paul M. Stevens, former president of the Southern Baptist Radio and Television Commission, made this truth come to life for me when in a sermon he imagined an interview with two leading apostles:

"I turn to the apostle Paul to say, 'Paul, I'm sorry. I can't understand. I'm a lost man, and I read about these things— that you once were a murderer and a blasphemer, that you disturbed others. Paul, how is it possible that your life was changed?' Paul begins to sing in his own way: 'What can wash away my sin?/Nothing but the blood of Jesus;/. . . Oh, precious is the flow/That makes me white as snow; . . . / Nothing but the blood of Jesus.' Simon Peter, how was it that you, a calloused sailor, a man of profanity who smelled of hard work and fish, who turned away from the things of God consistently, could suddenly become a great preacher? In his own way, Simon Peter sings: 'I stand amazed in the presence/ Of Jesus the Nazarene,/And wonder how he could love me,/A sinner, condemned, unclean./. . . How marvelous! how wonderful! Is my Savior's love for me!'"

The great thing about our gospel is not that it tells us that we are sinners, but there is victory over sin. Knowing Jesus Christ gives victory in life.

Some have the idea that Christianity and happiness live across the street from each other. In reality, they live in the same house. Purpose, peace, and joy are the direct outcome of the presence of Christ within a life. A victorious Christian life is the by-product of Christian maturity.

Jesus didn't come just to give us something so we won't fry when we die. He came to give us victory in this life. He kept saying to people, "I am come that they might have life, and that they might have it more abundantly" (John 10:10).

We have more to be happy about than anyone else in the world. Our Lord has forgiven our sins and placed them in the sea of his forgetfulness and put up a sign, "No Fishing Here."

When I was nineteen, I found the greatest kick in life is to know Jesus Christ. He has filled my life with joy and peace and purpose. And the kicks you have when you're a Christian don't kick back!

A few summers ago, it was my happy assignment to be involved in an evangelistic crusade in Dayton, Ohio. I was put into a motor hotel in downtown Dayton. On the courthouse lawn, just a few blocks away, was gathered a group of hippies. To this same crusade John LaNoue and Kaywin, his wife, brought a group of college students from the Texas Rio Grande Valley.

John is one of those mechanical geniuses who can make anything work. He fixed up an old panel truck, painted it white, and put in large letters on the side "BSU" for Baptist Student Union. As they would drive through those towns up East, people would look at that bus with the letters "BSU" on the side and say, "Those dumb Texans can't even spell BUS."

Well, those young people piled off that old bus and said to

the people on the courthouse lawn: "We're a bunch of religious fanatics from Texas, and we want to tell you about Christ." Five of those people became Christians, overjoyed at the life our Lord Christ had brought them.

There is yet a third thing the Scripture would tell us: when one is in Christ, he has victory over time. The game of life has a time limit. Just when a person thinks he is about to score the whistle blows, and the great referee announces that time has run out. Isn't this the tragedy of our lives—that just when one thinks he is ready to live, he must die? That when one is ready to really enjoy life, time runs out?

Time is the enemy. We can't escape it. We may look at time with thoughtless courage, making faces at it; or with reasoned courage, we may stand and endure what time will do. But it is always there waiting for us; and like beasts helplessly caught in traps of whirling clocks, we simply wait for whatever dreadful fate time will bring us.

When Christ came out of that grave, he said, "Cheer up, I've overcome the world." One of the things he meant was, "I have overcome time." Christ is timeless. When you belong to Jesus Christ, you're never really going to die!

What is the victory over sin, over time? Jesus Christ. And that same Christ is offering to you this victory. Hear him as he says, "To-day if ye will hear his voice, harden not your hearts" (Heb. 3:7). "Come unto me, . . . and I will give you rest" (Matt. 11:28).

Two contrasting works of poetry present in vivid fashion the fascinating fact that Jesus Christ makes all the difference in two worlds. The first is the well-known, oft-quoted "Invictus" by William Ernest Henley:

> Out of the night that covers me,
>   Black as the pit from pole to pole,

I thank whatever gods may be
  For my unconquerable soul.

In the fell clutch of circumstance
  I have not winced nor cried aloud.
Under the bludgeonings of chance
  My head is bloody but unbowed.

Beyond this place of wrath and tears
  Looms but the Horror of the shade,
And yet the menace of the years
  Finds, and shall find me unafraid.

It matters not how strait the gate,
  How charged with punishment the scroll,
I am the master of my fate;
  I am the captain of my soul.

It sounds brave, doesn't it? But the force of even this foolish bravery is quelled by the fact that the author of these lines, in his deep despondency, took his own life.

An unknown author has written the Christian's answer to "Invictus":

Out of the light that dazzles me,
  Bright as the sun from pole to pole,
I thank the God I know to be
  For Christ, the conqueror of my soul.

Since He's the sway of circumstance,
  I would not wince nor cry aloud
Under the rule which men call chance
  My head with joy is humbly bowed.

Beyond this place of sin and tears—
  That life with Him! And He's the aid
That, spite the menace of the years
  Keeps and shall keep me unafraid!

I have no fear though strait the gate,
  He cleared from punishment the scroll.
Christ is the master of my fate:
  Christ, the captain of my soul.

AUTHOR UNKNOWN

When you link your life by faith to Christ, you have victory over sin, victory in life, and victory over time. This is what the Bible means when it asserts, "Thanks be to God, which giveth us the victory through our Lord Jesus Christ" (1 Cor. 15:57).

15

Know the Ropes and You'll Be Free

Many years ago in a city on our nation's east coast there was a rope factory which manufactured the great docking halters for ships—those vital, giant ropes which anchored the ship to the docking place. Over the entrance way to that factory a message was painted, "The Worker in This Factory Weaves His Conscience into His Work—for Lives Are at Stake."

In the first century God had a man who literally wove his conscience, his life, his all into his work. When he wrote his letter to Rome, he was communicating with people he had never seen. He was willing to lay bare his heart so he could share God's truth, so he wrote:

I am under obligation both to Greeks and to barbarians, both to the wise and to the foolish. Thus, for my part, I am eager to preach the gospel to you also who are in Rome. For I am not ashamed of the gospel, for it is the power of God for salvation to every one who believes, to the Jew first and also to the Greek (Rom. 1:14-16, NASB).

And they knew Paul wore scars testifying to the validity of that statement.

On a post in that same factory producing those important anchor ropes was a bronze plaque containing the words of a poem entitled, "Ropes of Gold."

> Our lives must be anchored with golden
>   ropes
> That gives us purpose, meaning, hopes.
> Know the ropes. Know the ropes and
>   you'll be free.
> To know them not means slavery.
> What are those precious golden strands
> Holding freedom unknown in other lands?

AUTHOR UNKNOWN

Paul and that poet knew something we all need to learn. He knew the secret of a life, of a church, of a nation is found not in detachment but in commitment. When Paul said, "I am under a great obligation, a severe sense of duty to share this thing I know about Christ," he was not looking for pity or applause. He was explaining his power. This was a golden rope.

We like to sing in our church, "Blest be the tie that binds/ Our hearts in Christian love." We need to ponder those ties and seek not to be loosed from them, but to be more tightly bound by them. Herein lies freedom.

There is a very real sense in which faith is like the miraculous manna in the Old Testament. Remember how God provided them with that food, but only one day at a time. They tried to store it, get enough for a week or a month, or at least tomorrow because you can never tell when a "manna recession" might set in. But it wouldn't work. Yesterday's manna wouldn't keep. Don't make the comparison crawl on all fours, but faith is like that: not so much what you say you believe, but what you do because of what you really believe. When we come to that, yesterday's manna won't keep. This is a frightening thing about where we stand in a nation, in a city, in a church. We are enjoying the labors of others who have invested love and time and prayer (real praying is hard work) and their very lives into this effort to honor Christ and to build a good nation, to build a good city. And one generation of us could come along and blow it all. Yesterday's manna won't keep. What our nation, our city, and our church is and is becoming depends upon our relationships with God now and what kind of lives we live. That's why those "gold ropes" are important.

In looking at the letters God wrote through Paul to churches it is amazing how he emphasizes key factors, some things that matter much in the life of relationships of God's people.

A gold rope that holds people of God together and holds much of the power of the people of God is fellowship. In a prominent place somewhere in every letter Paul wrote to churches, he admonished them to cling tightly to the strong rope of fellowship. Romans is a theological letter. In this letter we are told why everyone in the world must have Christ, how everyone in the world can have Christ, why the Jews rejected Christ, and how they must have him, too. And now after these vital theological issues are answered he begins the fourteenth chapter by saying, "Now accept the one who is weak in faith" (Rom. 14:1, NASB).

The letter to the Corinthians was in reply to great problems. They had moral problems, bad ones. They had spiritual problems, such sinful, spiritual pride. But the first problem Paul attacked in that torn church was their fellowship problem. They were split four ways, arguing about, of all things, who their favorite preachers were. One group said, "We like Apollos. He's smart." Another asserted, "We like Simon Peter; he's strong." Still another bunch said, "We're Paul's people." And there was a proud gang who scoffed, "We won't have anything to do with any of you. We are of Christ." But Paul said, "You have broken the body of our Lord into many pieces" (see 1 Cor. 1:10-17). And he pled with them to mend the break in fellowship.

When he wrote to the Galatians, Paul taught: when a brother is overtaken in a sin, when he slips, don't laugh at him, don't criticize him. Help him. Love him. He needs you (Gal. 6:1). He admonished the Philippians: don't be selfish. Be humble. Think of others as better than yourselves (Phil. 2:3). To the Colossians he said, "Epaphras has told me the good news how the Holy Spirit has given you a great love for each other" (based on Col. 1:7-8). To the Thessalonians he wrote that their love was already strong toward all the Christian brothers throughout the whole nation. "We urge you, brethren, to excel still more" (1 Thess. 4:9-10, NASB).

Paul wrote to two young preachers. First Timothy is almost a manual on how to organize a church. In chapter 5, he told Timothy to teach the church to be caring, looking for those who need spiritual attention.

To Titus, the other preacher, Paul said: "Teach your people to live peacefully in this world. Tell them not to speak evil of anyone, but to be gentle and courteous to all." In a very personal letter to Philemon, Paul said, "I know how much you love and trust the Lord Christ, and I know how much you love and trust His people." There it is. *Fellowship* is one of the golden ropes. It is important to hold to it.

You've heard the expression, "We're all in the same boat." Oh, we are. And we Christians need to show the world around us that ship is seaworthy. It will stand up in life's storms. Let me share with you an indisputable, scientific fact about a boat: you can't sink half of one! On a ship you just can't sink the officer's quarters and have the enlisted men's part keep afloat, and vice versa.

A ship was way out at sea. Two Irish sailors were talking,

and one of them said, "The boiler's blown up! We're taking in water! The ship's going to sink!" The other fellow said, "Let her sink. She's not ours." Now that won't work. I've seen churches fail because someone thought they could sink someone else's part of the boat, and the whole thing went down.

Actually, Jesus tied two of those vital ropes together when he commanded, "A new commandment I give unto you, That ye love one another. . . . By this shall all men know that ye are my disciples, if ye have love one for another" (John 13:34-35). Now that's the big reason for fellowship, that all may know that we are his disciples. That's why Paul said, "I owe my love, my fellowship to you at Rome and all people everywhere because I am not ashamed of the gospel of Christ."

The second golden rope which brings a group of people together is an eye for the main thing—a vision which keeps our primary task in full view. We are to be sharing the gospel of Christ. The great problem with many modern Christian movements is not so much that they are wrong, but that they're taking away from the church's great assignment. People who truly love him have left his commandment to "go and make disciples" and spend their efforts trying to remake disciples already reached to fit their interpretation of the Scriptures.

Paul was an intellectual giant of the first century. He was also a highly spiritual, mystic man. After he met Christ he did not aim his efforts at an intellectually based defense of the gospel. Nor did he teach people to perform some spiritual trick to prove the reality of the presence of the Holy Spirit. Rather, he gave his life, going all over the world, telling a very simple story of how Jesus Christ wants to forgive and accept all who come to him by faith.

Sam Shoemate wrote some lines entitled "I Stand by the Door." "Others," he said, "seem to think it vital to delve deeply into the mysteries of the faith. But I stand by the door, helping people to get in." This must always be seen as each Christian's biggest job. "When the Holy Spirit has come upon you," said Christ in Acts 1:8, "you shall be My witnesses" (NASB).

The third strong rope is to keep aware that our confidence is in God. Paul was saying, "I owe my fellowship, my love, to the whole world." In Romans 1:16 he said: "I am not ashamed of the gospel of Christ: for it is the power of God unto salvation to every one that believeth." Without his power, it won't happen.

How do you explain the growth of a church? How do you account for things happening in the name of Christ? Without the presence of God there is no explanation. We cannot say that organization, hard work, or a number of factors have made things happen. God makes them happen. "Not by might, nor by power, but by my Spirit, saith the Lord" (Zech. 4:6).

I once served on a committee to select the leader of some two million Christians. When discussing in a meeting one day what kind of person we were looking for, someone suggested that he be a "self-confident" man. Now the one who made that suggestion was a godly person. I liked what I think he meant, but I did not like what he said. I suggested we reword that to say that we wanted a "God-confident" man. This is so vital to Christian fellowship. We have no reason to be confident in ourselves, but we have every reason to be confident in him.

I pray the following before almost every service in which I preach.

Lord, I thank you that I know you put me here and that you will help me preach for the sake of these dear people. And Father, I realize that if anything is going to happen in people's hearts today, you will be the One who makes it happen.

The golden ropes of "fellowship," an eye for what is vital, and total confidence in God anchor us to our calling.

Now the last lines of the poem:

> These, friends, are the "ropes of gold"
> That all our precious freedoms hold.
> To look around at a distant star,
> To look ahead to horizons far.
> To look upward through the dawn
> To trust in God and carry on.

16

Do You Think You're the Greatest?

Daniel 1—4

During the days of Daniel, if you had polled the people of Babylon asking, "Who is the greatest man who ever lived?" those people would have answered as one vast rehearsed choir. In four-part harmony they would have chanted a single name, "Nebuchadnezzar."

Many pages of ancient history and the first four chapters of Daniel reveal the unusual story of one of history's great leaders. Even the bizarre mind of Alfred Hitchcock could never conjure a mystery as strange as this one.

Nebuchadnezzar's story will probably never catch the eye of the Oscar chasers in Hollywood because by this world's standards, even its strictest ones, he was a pretty good guy. Yet he faced the severe judgment of God. Let's look hard at his story, for many of the best of today's men are like Nebuchadnezzar.

For forty-three years, Nebuchadnezzar ruled this vast and wealthy empire. There was never a threat to his throne. It was agreed by all that he was the ablest man of all Babylon.

During his long reign, the Egyptians were the only power to dare invade his territory, and they were soundly defeated. He kept his country militarily prepared.

This great king was not only a sound military leader but also a splendid negotiator. To the north and east he had established firm alliances with the Medes and Persians. During the last sixteen years of his reign he is described in Daniel 4:4 as being "at rest in my house and flourishing in my palace."

A requirement for the success of any leader is to bring about him the very best of leadership. Nebuchadnezzar was able to work with capable men, even when they did not share his opinions.

It is hard to visualize a Babylonian ruler putting up with that, but this king did want the best minds about him, and he found in the conquered city of Jerusalem four young men. They were not the same race as he. They did not share his same religious convictions.

Like most men, this king had his times of confronting God and viewing his faith in God. There came upon the king one night a strange and disturbing dream. He was troubled terribly by this dream. He couldn't sleep. Daniel 2:1 states that "sleep brake from him." He summoned all the wise men of his kingdom and told them that he was disturbed by this dream, and he wanted them to tell him what it meant.

A Chaldean wise man said: "Tell us the dream, O king, and we will show the interpretation." And the king said, "The thing is gone from me. You tell me both the dream and the interpretation" (author's translation). When it became apparent that they could not fill that demanding assignment, the king ordered that the unwise head of every wise man in his kingdom be severed from his body.

Daniel heard of this, prayed to God, and God revealed to Daniel the king's dream. Coming before Nebuchadnezzar, Daniel testified that the God of all gods had revealed this wisdom to him. He said that Nebuchadnezzar had seen in his dream an image of a strong and mighty being crushing empires and obliterating all who opposed him. Then Daniel said, "O king, you are in your position of power only because the God of heaven has given you your kingdom, but one day our God will set up a kingdom that shall never be destroyed: and it shall stand forever" (author's translation).

In chapter 2, verse 47, we read: "The king answered unto Daniel, and said, Of a truth it is, that your God is a God of gods, and a Lord of kings."

Like all too many men, King Nebuchadnezzar went back to his old way of life after the crisis was over. He was a worshiper of the pagan god Marduk. Daniel 3 records that the king had an image of this god put up in a place so that at the morning hour of prayer the rays of the sun would reflect on the gold.

Then the decree was sent out ordering that at the sounds of the "tinny" instruments that composed a Babylonian orchestra (This to us would sound terrible but sounded great to them.) every person would fall on his knees and bow before the image of Marduk.

Daniel's friends were brought before the angry king. He demanded to know why they would not bow before his image and boisterously asked, "Who is that God that shall deliver you out of my hands?" (Dan. 3:15). And these men answered,

O Nebuchadnezzar, we are not worried about what will happen to us. If we are thrown into the flaming furnace, our God is able to deliver us; and he will deliver us out of your hand, Your Majesty. But if he doesn't, please understand, sir, that even then we will never under any circumstances serve your gods or worship the golden image you have erected" (Dan. 3:16-18, author's translation).

Now the king was really hopping. The Bible states that he was "full of fury" (v. 19). He ordered that the furnace be heated seven times as hot as usual.

Those furnaces of Babylon were really interesting. They were heated by naphtha, which, as you well know, can make a most hot blaze. As was the cross in the first century, the stake at which people were tied and burned in the Dark Ages, and the gallows, gas chambers, and electric chairs of recent years, the furnace of Babylon was the method of execution. This was public punishment. Large, tall balconies were constructed so that one would look down into the flames to witness the victim being consumed in the fire.

In consternation, Nebuchadnezzar watched as some of his best men were consumed by the intense heat when they pushed Shadrach, Meshach, and Abednego into the flames. But suddenly, as he was watching, Nebuchadnezzar jumped up in amazement and exclaimed to his advisers:

"Didn't we throw three men into the blazing furnace?" "Yes," they said, "we did, indeed, Your Majesty." "Well, look!" Nebuchadnezzar shouted. "I see four men, unbound, walking around in the fire, and They aren't even hurt by the flames! And the fourth looks like a god!" Then Nebuchadnezzar came as close as he could to the open door of the flaming furnace and yelled: "Shadrach, Meshach, and Abednego, servants of the Most High God! Come out! Come here!" So they stepped out of the fire (Dan. 3:24-26, author's translation).

Then Nebuchadnezzar said, "Blessed be the God of Shadrach, Meshach, and Abednego, for He sent his angel to deliver his trusting servants when they defiled the king's commandment, and were willing to die rather than serve or worship any god except their own" (v. 28, author's translation). Once again, he paid homage to God, but he did not give his life to him.

God deals again with the king. One day Nebuchadnezzar called Daniel before him saying:

I had a dream. I saw a tree, strong and mighty and big enough to be seen from the ends of the earth. It bore much fruit and gave much protection.

Then suddenly a holy one came down from heaven and cried,

"Cut it down, cut off his branches, and scatter his fruit. But leave the stump of his roots in the ground; let it be wet with the dew of heaven, and let him have the same existence as an animal in the field. Let his heart be no longer the heart of a man, but of a beast. Let him know that the Most High ruleth in the kingdom of man and giveth it to whomever he will" (4:5-17, author's translation).

When Daniel heard the words, he was so sad he did not speak for an hour. Finally Nebuchadnezzar prompted him to say what must be said.

"O king," said Daniel, "you are that tree. You have grown so strong and mighty and you are known to the ends of the earth. But all those things you saw in the vision will happen to you" (author's translation).

Earnestly, Daniel begged his king to make restitution for his sins, but to no avail. One year later, King Nebuchadnezzar was walking on the balcony of his palace. He looked out over the beauty of his beloved capital city, much of which had been either built or bettered during his reign. The wall around the city had been made much stronger. Forty miles of wall it was around the city—sixty- to seventy-feet high and thirty-feet wide.

He could see the restored tower of Babel and the famous tower of Ziggurat. Two hundred yards square at its base and two hundred yards tall this monument was larger and taller than the Washington Memorial. He saw the giant recreational reservoir he had built and the fabulous gardens of Babylon. There was the vast stone bridge over the Euphrates, an engineering feat that to this day baffles the experts.

He saw all this and proudly said:

"Is this not Babylon the great, which I myself have built as a royal residence by the might of my power and for the glory of my majesty?"

While the word was in the king's mouth, a voice came from heaven, saying, "King Nebuchadnezzar, to you it is declared: sovereignty has been removed from you, and you will be driven away from mankind, and your dwelling place will be with the beasts of the field. You will be given grass to eat like cattle, and seven periods of time will pass over you, until you recognize that the Most High is ruler over the realm of mankind, and bestows it on whomever He wishes."

Immediately the word concerning Nebuchadnezzar was fulfilled; and he was driven away from mankind and began eating grass like cattle, and his body was drenched with the dew of heaven, until his hair had grown like eagles' feathers and his nails like birds' claws.

But at the end of that period I, Nebuchadnezzar, raised my eyes toward heaven, and my reason returned to me, and I blessed the Most High and praised and honored Him who lives forever;

For His dominion is an everlasting dominion,
And His kingdom endures from generation to generation.
And all the inhabitants of the earth are accounted as nothing,
But He does according to His will in the host of heaven
And among the inhabitants of earth;
And no one can ward off His hand
Or say to Him, "What hast Thou done?"

At that time my reason returned to me. And my majesty and splendor were restored to me for the glory of my kingdom, and my counselors and my nobles began seeking me out; so I was re-established in my sovereignty, and surpassing greatness was added to me.

Now I Nebuchadnezzar praise, exalt, and honor the King of heaven, for all His works are true and His ways just, and He is able to humble those who walk in pride (vv. 30-37, NASB).

17

Can You Read the Writing on the Wall?

Daniel 5

Recent news releases from England told of a proposed movie which would portray the life of our Lord Christ as a lust-filled orgy. What a tragic testimony to sin's perverting power, that a man would use the mind God gave him to conjure such a project! Even more tragic is the estimation in the minds of those investing in the movie that the American public will buy it.

It brings to mind this Old Testament scene in which a Babylonian king, in drunken distastefulness, desecrates the sacred vessels taken from the Temple in Jerusalem. The episode warns that God always reaches a point that "enough is enough."

On this occasion the government heads of the vast Babylonian Empire were gathered in the capital city. While they were there, King Belshazzar made elaborate plans to entertain them. Belshazzar was a swinging king. He seemed to care more for parties than politics. He didn't know a great deal about running a government, but he had a splendid reputation for his ability to throw a party. Of course, a reputation like that must be protected. No party must end without an unusual twist, some bizarre happening that leaves the people buzzing. This current demand to entertain a thousand of his leaders had stumped him. Finally he got it! How funny it would be, he thought, to bring out those sacred gold and silver vessels his father had taken in Jerusalem and conclude his banquet by drinking a final toast to all the Babylonian pagan idols from these vessels dedicated to the worship of Jehovah.

When all had consumed enough wine to tax their total tankage capacity, these sacred vessels were brought in and passed around. They drank wine from containers dedicated to the worship of God, while they praised the gods of gold and silver, brass, iron, and wood.

God didn't think much of that. With total disrespect for decor and the dignitaries present, God painted a message on the wall of that palace banquet hall. In the last chapter I talked before of the architectural genius of Nebuchadnezzar, Belshazzar's father. This party took place in a most elaborate, beautiful building. God is never impressed primarily with people's projects, but rather with the people. Clever arrangements of stone and glass are not nearly so important as the character of the people within. The capital city of Babylon was impressive—the beautiful gardens, a giant recreational reservoir, the restored tower of Babylon, the two-hundred-yard-tall tower of Ziggurat, the giant wall, plus the capitol buildings—but what dazzled the world looked like a ghetto to God. For within the walls of that city resided a godless people. Sin had done its deteriorating work. When God looked at Babylon, he was not impressed. He saw the slums of the souls of its people.

So God smeared the palace walls with a message of judgment. But a now sobered and frightened Belshazzar couldn't read it. He didn't know the Hebrew language. It is not too fanciful, my friend, to state that the writing is on the wall today, but so many cannot read it. They've never learned the mother tongue of the kingdom of God. The language of righteousness and reverence is foreign rhetoric to them.

However, Belshazzar sought someone who could read the handwriting of God. It is imperative that those who know the

Lord, who understand his instructions, keep themselves known and visible. People who understand the words of God will always be in demand.

Daniel came into that frenzied scene and read aloud the four words, "Mene, mene, tekel, upharsin"—numbered, numbered, weighed, divided. You have been weighed in the balances and found wanting; your kingdom is gone. Before the night was ended, Cyrus' forces had attacked; Belshazzar was slain, and Darius was given the kingdom.

The handwriting on that ancient wall was indelibly inscribed. In fact, the message is for you and me. Its truths are self-evident in this hour.

Truth number one: You'd best not play games with Almighty God. He is in charge. Belshazzar thought God was weak and unable to do anything. After all, weren't the people who called themselves "God's Chosen People" his slaves? He not only had the sacred vessels from the Temple at Jerusalem in his possession, he also had Jerusalem. *Surely this God must be powerless,* mused Belshazzar, *or he wouldn't allow this to happen.*

At this point you and I are prone to play a dangerous game called "If I Were God." Whenever we feel tempted to tell God he's running things all wrong, we'd best remind ourselves that he has placed Christians in his sales department, not administration. We are called to be his witnesses, not his advisers.

God's anger was mightily roused by Belshazzar's irreverent misuse of containers dedicated to his worship. Perhaps as you read this story you find yourself also shocked at this unkingly, crude act of unholy gall. Yet, this is probably a sin you commit daily. You see, all those tools of worship in the Temple in Jerusalem were symbols of something. They were merely images or pictures of a real counterpart.

How does God interpret the word *vessel* to you and me? In

Acts 9:15 Ananias is understandably hesitant to seek out Saul of Tarsus. He is told by God, "Go ahead, for I have decided to use him as 'a chosen instrument of Mine, to bear My name before the Gentiles,'" (NASB). In 1 Thessalonians 4:4 we are told that, as vessels or instruments of God, we are to keep ourselves clean.

Paul wrote to Timothy: "In any big household there are naturally not only gold and silver vessels but wooden and earthenware utensils as well. Some are used for the highest purposes and some for the lowest. If a man keeps himself clean from the contamination of evil he will be a vessel used for honorable purposes, dedicated and serviceable for the use of the master of the household" (2 Tim. 2:21, Phillips).

How I hope you catch the thrust of that! You and I are God's vessels. He intends to fill us with himself, to pour out from us his blessings upon the world. To fill a vessel so designed with the junk, liquor, lust, and corruption of this world is a sin God does not take lightly!

In this same vein, Paul writes to the sinful Christians of Corinth: "Do you not know that you are a temple of God, and that Spirit of God dwells in you? If any man destroys the temple of God, God will destroy him, for the temple of God is holy, and that is what you are" (3:16-17, NASB).

When you and I ignore this sobering fact, like Belshazzar, we are inviting judgment and destruction. Don't play games with Almighty God.

Lesson number two: We ought to learn from past mistakes. Belshazzar grew up in the home of King Nebuchadnezzar, his father. Nebuchadnezzar was taught, the hard way, to recognize God as his source of power, wisdom, blessing, and life. Belshazzar had seen his father proudly boast of his independence. Ignoring God, he had proclaimed himself a self-made man. For his sinful pride he was punished with seven years of insane agony, at the end of which he humbly confessed: "Now I Nebuchadnezzar praise, exalt, and honor the King of heaven, for all His works are true and His ways just, for He is able to humble those who walk in pride" (Dan. 4:37, NASB). Belshazzar saw all that and heard his father make that confession. Daniel 5:17-21 records that Daniel told the same story over again that night to Belshazzar. Then verse 22 reads: "Yet you, his son, Belshazzar, have not humbled your heart, even though you knew all this" (NASB).

It is painfully amazing how people are not able to learn from the mistakes of others. What a testimony to the moral blindness of mankind that most alcoholics come from the homes of alcoholics. That children from broken homes are most likely to experience divorce themselves. How strange it is that, in so many ways, people watch other people get burned, cry with pain, suffer, carry scars, and then go and stick their hands in the same fire.

It is terribly appalling that we read so much history and don't learn from it. It is easy to learn that, since the dawn of history, there has been no less than twenty-two civilizations which have risen and fallen; and, when you go and look for the reasons and classify the reasons, they are notorious in their similarity. The best historians keep coming up with some four to six categories. Now think about this. It is historically documented that for these reasons previous civilizations failed:

1. They lost their religious convictions and flaunted basic morality.

2. They became obsessed with sex.

3. They debased their money of its intrinsic value and let inflation run rampant.

4. Honest work ceased to be a virtue.

5. Respect for law disintegrated, and violence became an

accepted method of achieving individual and group desires.

6. They reached the point that their citizens were no longer
willing to be soldiers and fight for the defense of their nation.
They resorted to paid mercenaries or tried to buy off their
attackers.

While we have not gone past the point of no return, America
has traveled dangerous distances down all six of those roads to
ruin. Belshazzar refused to learn from his father's experience
what no nation has learned from history: When these sins
begin their corruptive course, we must either go down to our
knees in repentance or be driven to our knees in defeat.

Lesson number three: The handwriting on the wall warns of
judgment. Four words appeared on that wall. The crux of the
message was, "Weighed and found wanting."

Had this news not come in such a shocking way, Belshazzar
would have argued the findings. He might well have replied,
"What do you mean, 'weighed on the scales'? What scales? I
have always made my own scales, set my own standards to
measure my worth."

You do this, don't you? I hear it all the time. "I do the best I
can. I'm an honest man. I work hard." Comments like these
come from men who manufacture their own scales, weigh
themselves, then decide that they may not be perfect, but
they'll do.

Hear carefully this word from heaven. One day you will
stand before Almighty God, not as you have invented him in
your mind but as he really is. You will be judged by his
standards, not yours. You won't get to take your scales to the
judgment; you'll have to weigh on his.

That wealthy farmer of Luke 12 was congratulating himself
on his wisdom and success only to be called foolish and a
failure by God. He had been living as though time were

eternity and eternity only the brief digit of time. He thought he could measure his value by how much his grain weighed, but he was using the wrong scales. "Weighed in the balances, and found wanting."

We have already been weighed on God's scales, and you and I are found wanting. This is what the Bible means in stating: "For all have sinned, and come short of the glory of God" (Rom. 3:23).

At this point we begin to understand the gospel. Like Paul, we say in despair: "O wretched man that I am! who shall deliver me from the body of this death?" (Rom. 7:24). And our despair can be changed to delight. "I thank God through Jesus Christ our Lord" (v. 25). When invited, Christ climbs on the scales with us and makes up the difference.

He gives his righteousness when we have none of our own.

18

Free Indeed!

John 8:26-31

Is there anything more desirable than freedom? It is a great day when anyone is set free. Freedom is at stake in the struggle for supremacy and world dominion. Yet, I fear that neither side thinks enough about it. Our enemies don't think about freedom because they've never experienced it. They don't know what it is. We are so prone to take it for granted and misuse it and thereby lose the thrill of it. We have been willing, as Americans, to fight to preserve our freedom. We all need to remember the words of Dwight Eisenhower, "A soldier's pack, in the final choice, is not as heavy as a prisoner's chain." Freedom is our greatest possession.

And it is our heaviest responsibility. Freedom calls for responsible living. Irresponsible use of freedom always leads to the loss of freedom. Drive a car irresponsibly, and you soon lose the freedom to drive a car. You can live as a citizen irresponsibly and eventually lose the freedom of responsible citizenship.

The responsibility of freedom is to preserve it. There is nothing you can lose more quickly than freedom. As the framers of our constitution emerged from the meeting room, someone stopped Benjamin Franklin and asked, "What have you given us?" He replied, "A republic, if you know how to keep it."

We can never keep freedom unless we guarantee the same

freedom for everyone. The quickest way to lose freedom is for some to assume the right to more freedom than others.

Many disturbing things are being said in the name of freedom. Strange statements are made about freedom of morality and freedom of speech. So much of what is being called "freedom" today is nothing more than selfish, often childish, irresponsibility. So it is vital that we understand what freedom really is.

The eighth chapter of John gives us good guidance in understanding freedom. Our Lord was attending the Feast of Tabernacles. As they lighted that golden celebration to signify the light that guided them in the wilderness, Jesus said, "I am the light of the world" (v. 12). This set off a tremendous debate between Jesus and the religious leaders. Out of that debate emerged some significant findings. They were ignorant of truth. Though they claimed liberty, they were not free at all. They blinded themselves to Jesus Christ. They chose to ignore the truth about him. They depended on their ancestry, on their external keeping of laws, and they were not free at all.

Here is the essential truth. Freedom is a spiritual thing. It cannot be judged by appearances. One can be free when he looks like a slave, and he can be a slave when it looks to all the world like he's free. Freedom is a spiritual thing.

Thomas Jefferson understood this. "The liberty we claim is a gift of God," he said. "Government may take liberty away from people like, on occasion, it takes life away from people; but, only God can give either liberty or life." That's what Jesus was saying: "Ye shall know the truth, and the truth shall make you free. . . . If the Son therefore shall make you free, ye shall be free indeed" (John 8:32-36).

Freedom is a spiritual thing. Some talk about "freedom of morality" as though being free means having a license to be immoral. Yet, each act of immorality makes you less free and more a slave to sin. What is the worth of freedom of worship if there is no God in your life to worship? What is the worth of freedom of speech if you have nothing really important to say? Real freedom means you are free to be the best you can be, to say the best, and to worship the highest One.

This freedom does not come by education. In a colossal disregard of context this line "Ye Shall Know the Truth, and the Truth Shall Make You Free" has been engraved on the portals of many a university in America. Now it is true that God is the author of all truth, but to have only academic truth is not to be free because our problem is much more than mere ignorance.

Freedom is not a matter of inheritance. These people with whom Jesus talked thought so. "We be Abraham's seed," they said, "and were never in bondage to any man" (v. 33). There is something admirable in that spirit. Yet they were caught up in a bondage they would not admit. It is a bondage all of us share with them. To all of us comes God's Word: "You shall know the truth, and the truth shall make you free" (v. 32, NASB). If the Son sets you free, you will be free indeed.

This is the real freedom because it set us free from our deepest slavery.

If any of you would dare say with the Pharisees, "I am no slave. I am in bondage to no one," he asks, "What about your sin? I tell you," said Jesus, "anyone who sins is a slave to sin." The bondage of sin is a slavery worse than any that Rome could impose upon a person. What personal tragedy is contained in the truth of John 8:34?

Seneca said, "Who is free if sin is our master? One is a slave to lust, another is the slave of avarice, and another is the slave of an ungodly ambition. All of us are the slaves of fear." He could have said all of us are the slaves of sin. When a sinful habit begins to spin its web about us, it is so innocent and frail.

It only tickles, and we are sure we could snap its hold in a minute. But what starts as a spider's web becomes a logging chain, and we are in bondage.

I have had leaders of large enterprises, men able to control millions of dollars yet unable to control their passions, come and say, "Preacher, what on earth is wrong with me?"

Gordon Clinard was called by one who said, "I've got things wrong with me that all the doctors in the world can't fix"—the bondage of sin.

Some who like to discount the language of God have called human failure "a lack of authentic personhood." That's close. One word translated *sin* in your Bible means "missing the mark" or "not being the person you were made to be." Being a slave to sin means you never know why you exist. There is never a fulfilling purpose for living. What greater bondage than that of an unfulfilled destiny. Jesus Christ is our destiny. He can set you free, free to be what you'll *never* be without him.

One ancient teacher criticized Christianity as being made up of the "ragtag and bobtails of society." To that another answered, "It is true that Christ takes those others would count worthless, stands them on their feet, and allows them to look into the face of God." You are never free until you find your reason for being here.

Only Christ can free you from the deeper bondage of the fear of death. In verse 51 he declares, "If anyone keeps My word he shall never see death" (NASB). All of our days are shadowed by the cloud of death. It is one of the basic unavoidables. We may try to ignore it, but it grimly reminds of its presence. We may deny it, but not for long. The Word of God declares, "It is appointed unto men once to die, but after this the judgment" (Heb. 9:27). Who is not held slave by the fear of death? One whose life is Christ's. That person has defeated death. In the coliseum Caesar would pound his fist on the arm of his throne asking, "Why aren't these Christians afraid to die?" Because of Christ, Paul climaxes 1 Corinthians 15: "O death, where is thy sting? O grave, where is thy victory? The sting of death is sin; and the strength of sin is the law. But thanks be to God, which gives us the victory through our Lord Jesus Christ" (1 Cor. 15:55-57). In his last days he wrote to Timothy: "The time of my departure is at hand. I have fought a good fight, I have finished my course, I have kept the faith: Henceforth there is laid up for me a crown of righteousness, which the Lord, the righteous judge, shall give me at that day: and not to me only, but unto all them also that love his appearing" (2 Tim. 4:6-8).

How great it is to be set free from the fear of death in Christ Jesus. "You shall know the truth, and the truth shall make you free. . . . If therefore the Son shall make you free, you shall be free indeed" (John 8:32-36, NASB).

Now hear this about real freedom. It comes when you choose the best slavery. One of life's most important lessons is to learn well that there is no such thing as absolute, unconditional freedom. This is a mistake being made by too many today.

During a rush-hour time, we approached a busy intersection in our city. It took us ten full minutes to get close enough to see what had caused the gigantic traffic jam. It was not an accident or a broken water main. It was simply that the traffic light was not working, and no one was there to direct the traffic. At that point I realized we shouldn't call those things "stop" lights; they are "go" lights. Without their direction we are slowed down considerably.

A Czechoslovakian grandmother had just arrived in New York City. She stepped out in the street and was jerked from the path of an onrushing city bus by a friendly man who said,

"Not against the lights, Grandmother. Not against the lights." In dismay she replied, "But I thought this was a free country!" It is a false idea of freedom to suppose you can do anything you want to do without any restraint.

There is no absolute freedom physically. You just can't go to Canada if you go south. You have to go north.

There is no absolute freedom socially. My freedom ends where your rights begin.

There are two kinds of freedom. There is a false freedom that does what it wants to do. There is a true freedom that does what it ought to do. The prodigal son thought he was free when he got all that money and broke away from his father's restraint. But the more he did what he liked, the less he liked what he did. He was not free at all. He was a prisoner of his passions. Every time his passion called, he heeled like the dog he was. Then he understood that freedom's only choice is to choose our own prison. We will be enslaved by something. He understood that at last and said, "I will choose the best slavery, my father's slavery. 'I will arise and go,' and I will say, 'make me as one of thy hired servants'" (Luke 15:18-19).

All of us are like a train. We are free only as we stay on the track. We will have freedom only as we fulfill our destiny. Destiny for you and me is Jesus Christ. That's it. "If therefore the Son shall make you free, you shall be free indeed" (NASB).

Paul found that freedom. It is his dominant theme, his most persistent witness, and his abiding testimony: "For to me to live is Christ" (Phil. 1:21). "I am crucified with Christ: nevertheless I live; yet not I, but Christ liveth in me" (Gal. 2:20). A favorite title for himself was, "Paul, a servant of Jesus Christ."

The only freedom you and I will ever know is in complete surrender to Jesus Christ. In verse 31 we read: "To those Jews who had believed Him," Jesus said, "If you abide in My word, then you are truly disciples of Mine" (NASB). The sentence construction here does not speak of saving faith. It simply means they understood what he said, and they were attracted to him. Our Lord's answer warns that freedom is not found in nominal belief in Jesus but in absolute discipleship.

We must pray with George Matheson, "Lord make me a slave, and then I'll be free." William Temple was right, "What we need is to be delivered from the freedom which is perfect bondage into the bondage which is perfect freedom."

In Poland today people are beginning to say aloud their dreams of freedom. They are daring to wonder what it would be like to make choices about work and life-style. In the United States of America we give thanks to God for freedom much of the rest of the world cannot imagine, yet there is a yearning in your heart for real freedom. Freedom from life's deepest bondage. Freedom from sin. Freedom to be yourself, the real person God made you to be. Freedom from fear, even freedom from death itself. Jesus Christ gives that freedom. Hear him say: "If the Son sets you free, then you will be really free" (John 8:36, GNB).

Note

Since this cover was designed, Dr. Frank Pollard, author of this book, *After You've Said I'm Sorry*, and *The Bible and Your Life*, has assumed the presidency of Golden Gate Baptist Theological Seminary, Mill Valley, California.